Circular Walks
in
North Devon
including EXMOOR

Simone Stanbrook-Byrne
and
James Clancy

CULM VALLEY PUBLISHING

Published by:
Culm Valley Publishing Ltd
Yarde Down Farm,
Silverton, Devon
EX5 4DG, UK
Tel: +44(0)1392 881513
E-mail: info@culmvalleypublishing.co.uk
Website: www.culmvalleypublishing.co.uk

First published 2013, reprinted with revisions 2016

ISBN 978-1-907942-09-9 paperback

British Library Cataloguing-in-Publication Data
A catalogue record for this book is available from the British Library

Typeset by Culm Valley Publishing Ltd

Printed and bound on FSC approved paper by:
Ashford Colour Press Ltd, Gosport, Hants PO13 0FW

Front cover image: Stepping stones across the River Heddon (Walk 5)
Back cover image: Admiring the Exmoor coastline (Walk 7)

All images used in this book are available as cards and prints from Culm Valley Publishing

Contents

Introduction

Writing this walking guide has been very enjoyable. We've walked through fabulous views, found hidden paths, enjoyed country inns with open fires or sunny gardens, discovered new places and rediscovered some old ones.

On any walk common sense must prevail: be properly shod and take care where you put your feet, be prepared for any kind of weather, take food and first aid supplies with you and make sure someone knows where you're going. Mobile phones are often useless in the middle of nowhere.

We feel it's important that you take the **correct OS map** with you plus a **compass** (where advised) and are conversant with their use. Our sketch maps are precisely that – sketches – and are for rough guidance only and not necessarily to scale.

You know you've had a good day's walking when you get home safely at the end of it.

Follow the countryside code:
www.naturalengland.org.uk/ourwork/enjoying/countrysidecode/default.aspx

Our grateful thanks to:

Norman Govier for historical input on North Molton and Yarde Down walks.
Pat Wakeman and Simon Tootell for information on and photos of Poltimore House.
Penelope Rooth and Paul O'Neill from Waterloo House, Lynton.
Nic, Ella and William Clancy & Tony Byrne for listening to us waxing lyrical about places they haven't seen.

Disclaimer

Points that should be borne in mind on any route:

Public footpaths can be legally re-routed from the path shown on the map. In such cases they are usually clearly signposted. Where this has happened before the time of writing it has been noted in the text.

Most public footpaths are on private land. Please respect this.

Don't be surprised to find livestock grazing on public footpaths – and treat all animals with caution and respect.

If a field is planted with crops across a footpath, provision is usually made around the edge of the field.

Landmarks can change: trees and hedges may disappear; streams can dry up in warm weather or flood after heavy rain; stiles turn into gates and vice versa; fences appear where previously there was no boundary. Even views are different as the seasons progress. In such cases a modicum of common sense must be exercised – in conjunction with the OS map.

Public footpaths are at times blocked by barbed wire etc. Should this render the route impassable find the shortest detour around that section.

Please leave gates as you find them and if you have to climb them do so at the hinge end where it's stronger.

Exercise caution on wet stiles – they can be extremely slippery.

Take all your rubbish with you, please don't damage anything during the walk and please don't pick plants.

Please keep your dogs under proper control.

We hope that you enjoy these walks without mishap, but urge you to exercise common sense at all times. Neither the authors nor Culm Valley Publishing Ltd accepts responsibility for any misadventure that may occur during, or arise from, these walks and suggested routes.

Walk Locations

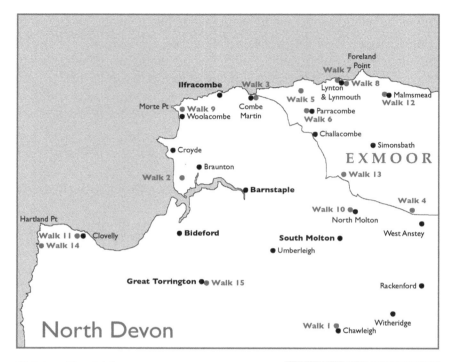

Foreland Point
Walk 7
Ilfracombe · Walk 3 · Lynton · Walk 8
Walk 5 · & Lynmouth · Malmsmead
Morte Pt · Walk 9 · Combe · Walk 12
Woolacombe · Martin · Parracombe
Walk 6
Challacombe
Croyde · Simonsbath
EXMOOR
Braunton
Walk 2 · Walk 13
Barnstaple
Walk 10 · Walk 4
Hartland Pt · North Molton
Walk 11 · Clovelly · Bideford · South Molton · West Anstey
Walk 14 · Umberleigh
Great Torrington · Walk 15
Rackenford
North Devon · Walk 1 · Witheridge
Chawleigh

Near Crow Point (Walk 2)

Chawleigh

Distance: 4½ miles / 7¼km

A lovely walk through river valleys and woodlands, climbing to an historic settlement. Occasionally the way follows very quiet lanes. Part of the walk crosses a stream and the route can be very wet unless we're having a dry summer so wellies are advised. There are a few steady climbs.

Map: OS Explorer 127, South Molton & Chulmleigh 1:25 000

Start point: From outside The Earl of Portsmouth public house. Grid ref: SS712125. Postcode: EX18 7HL

Directions to start: Chawleigh lies 18 miles south east of Great Torrington. It can be reached by taking the A377 to Eggesford and then the B3042 which passes through the village

Parking: On street parking near The Earl of Portsmouth public house

Public Transport: Bus operators that serve Chawleigh are Beacon Bus and Turners Tours. Timetables available online at www.travelinesw.com. Nearest railway station is Eggesford (2 miles)

Distance: 4½ miles

Refreshments: Earl of Portsmouth, Chawleigh, 01769 580204; Royal Oak Inn, Chawleigh, 01769 580427

Toilets: In Chawleigh

Nearby places to stay: Old Bakehouse, South Molton St, Chulmleigh, 01769 580074; Royal Oak Inn, Chawleigh, 01769 580427

Nearby places of interest: Cobbaton Combat Collection, Chittlehampton, 01769 540740; Quince Honey Farm, North Road, South Molton, 01769 572401

Possible birds include: Blackbird, blue tit, chaffinch, dunnock, goldfinch, great spotted woodpecker, jay, linnet, magpie, mistle thrush, pheasant, starling, woodpigeon, wren

Authors' tip: If you have time visit the nearby town of Chulmleigh, a very attractive place with good places to eat and an annual summer fair which has taken place since 1253

The walk starts outside the Earl of Portsmouth, taking the lane downhill (signed for Cheldon and Gidley Arms). You soon pass Leaches House, with the crest of the Earl of Portsmouth (who once owned the Manor and much of the land hereabouts) on its porch, and beyond this a small crossroads. Continue ahead for 1km on the lane out of the village, after

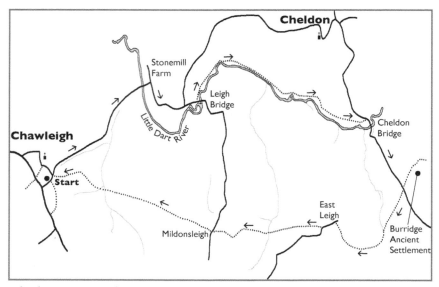

which you cross the Little Dart River at Stonemill Bridge. A short way beyond this, at Stonemill Cross, turn right towards Cheldon.

Continue for 350m to cross another small bridge. Ignore a left turn for Cheldon and keep ahead towards Lapford. You quickly reach Leigh Bridge and beyond this there is a public footpath signed left off the lane beside the river. Take this. The main body of the river is to your right now with a stream to the left.

The path broadens to enter a field, walk ahead through the field with the meandering river over to the right. At the end of the field pass through a gate and continue under trees, river still to the right. Emerge into another field and keep ahead through this in the same direction as before following the left boundary. You pass a stand of trees to your right, keep going in the same direction beyond them, climbing slightly to pass through a tree-topped boundary less than 200m further on.

Beyond this boundary the path may become quite wet as it veers slightly right towards a stand of oak trees and continues beyond them, passing a few more solitary trees, to find a yellow-arrowed stile at the end of the field. At the stile the river is about 30m to your right. Beyond the stile follow the trodden path between trees, there is a house up to your left and the path brings you out to a lane. Turn right.

Follow the lane as is it ascends to cross Cheldon Bridge and keep going up, passing West Burridge on your left and continuing for another 50m to where you find footpaths on both sides of the lane. Our way lies to the right but first go left on the path signed for Burridge Ancient Settlement, a diversion of less than 200m. The track rises to pass through a gate bringing you into the area of the settlement. Once you've pondered the history return down to the lane and take the footpath opposite, crossing the field in the direction shown by the fingerpost to meet the outside corner of some woodland 150m away.

Here you find a yellow-arrowed gate. Pass through and follow the track beyond, going downhill under the trees and passing an arrowed post on the way. Just over 150m from entering the woodland the path descends to cross a confluence of streams. A yellow-arrowed post points you right, across the stream, to another post less than 50m away which directs you

Woodland path by the Little Dart River

Attractive trees adorn the meadows alongside the Little Dart River

left. Pick your way through this aqueous chicane, don't sit down in the mud and be glad you've got wellies on (we did tell you!). If you're doing this in summer you may wonder what all the fuss is about.

Beyond the water follow the clear track as directed by the arrow, stream now to your left and rising ground to your right. After almost 500m you reach the lane at East Leigh. Go left along it for less than 150m and as the lane bends left take the track to the right. In 50m the track bends right, leave it here, passing through a farm gate into a field. Walk across the field in the direction of the arrow to a gate at the far side. Again go straight across, enjoying the views around you, to a yellow-arrowed footpath gate in the far boundary, which is set slightly low down so you may not see it until you're almost there.

From this gate cross the next field to another gate, 100m away in the opposite boundary. From here follow the direction of the yellow arrow for 150m across the next field to the outside corner of a tree-lined boundary where you find an arrowed gate (this gate is about 50m beyond a solitary tree in the field you're crossing).

Go through the gate and walk away from it on the trodden path, which vaguely follows the line of the right hand boundary of this small field (which was rather overgrown at the time of writing). The path bears right to an arrowed post pointing you out of the field along a track. This leads to a gate onto a lane, turn left along it and within a few metres go right off the lane on a concrete drive between Mildonsleigh and The Granary. The concrete ends, keep going on the track to reach a gate where there is an attractively-framed view towards the church tower in Chawleigh.

Beyond the gate veer slightly left down the field to find a post with a yellow arrow, guiding you past a lovely big oak with its own arrow on the trunk to a gate behind the tree. Go through here and follow the direction of the arrow down a narrow path – if the trees aren't in full leaf you will be heading for the church tower at this point. Descend to an arrowed post pointing right to another post that directs you left to cross a stream. Beyond the stream climb the stile and walk ahead up the hillside beyond. The path climbs and bears right to enter a field. Go through the field with the hedge on your left and good views to the right.

Heading back to Chawleigh

This left boundary brings you to a fencepost with an arrow directing you along a track out of the field. Go through a gate and follow the drive past Blackwalls Cottages. You pass Leaches Farm on the left and emerge at the lane. Turn left to retrace your steps the short distance back to the village centre.

Burridge Settlement

Probably dating from before the Romans this ancient place would have been a protected area in which our ancestors led their lives. Surrounded by banks and a ditch, the broad, open area was guarded against possible marauders with entrances at either end. The track passing the settlement is likely to have  been part of a network of routes that criss-crossed England and were used for trade etc.

The Little Dart River

Braunton Burrows & the Great Field

Distance: 7.2 miles / 11.6km

This flat, easy-to-follow walk has much to offer. Rich in history, the area is also superb for wildlife. Braunton Burrows is the largest sand dune system in the country and is a UNESCO Biosphere Reserve, hosting a great diversity of plant and invertebrate life. It also offers excellent bird watching opportunities along the estuary. The walk follows easy paths but it can be rather muddy after continued wet weather. The stretch to the wreck is tide-dependent but is 'there and back again' so can be missed out if impassable. Part of the Burrows is a military training area but the route of the walk shouldn't be troubled by this.

Map: Outdoor Leisure 139: Bideford, Ilfracombe & Barnstaple 1:25 000

Start point: Sandy Lane Car Park. Grid ref: SS463350. Postcode: EX33 2NU

Directions to start: Access from Braunton on lanes from either the A361 or B3231

Parking: In Sandy Lane Car Park as per start point above

Public Transport: Bus companies that operate in the Braunton area are Stagecoach Devon and Filers Travel. Timetables available online at www.travelinesw.com. Nearest railway station is Barnstaple (6 miles)

Distance: 7.2 miles (includes excursion to wrecked boat)

Refreshments: The Williams Arms, Wrafton, 01271 812360; Wild Thyme Café, 5 Caen Shopping Centre, Caen Field, Braunton, 01271 815191

Toilets: Rather grim-looking portaloo in Sandy Lane Car Park

Nearby places to stay: The Brookfield, South Street, Braunton, 01271 812382; Kingsacre House, 66 Saunton Road, Braunton, 01271 812097

Nearby places of interest: Braunton & District Museum, The Bakehouse Centre, Caen Street, 01271 816688; Museum of British Surfing, The Yard, Caen Street, Braunton, 01271 815155

Possible birds include: Blackbird, buzzard, carrion crow, chaffinch, curlew, dunlin, goldfinch, great spotted woodpecker, grey heron, gulls of various type, house sparrow, lapwing, linnet, little egret, magpie, mallard, moorhen, mute swan, oystercatcher, redshank, robin, rook, common sandpiper, shelduck, song thrush, starling, teal, woodpigeon

Authors' tip: If you are in anyway ornithologically-minded ensure you take binoculars on this walk. The mixture of dune, estuary, marsh and river habitats ensure that a variety of birds will be seen, with sighting of occasional rarities

---

Leave the car park by the vehicular entrance and turn right along the broad track, walking away from the lane by which you arrived. Beyond

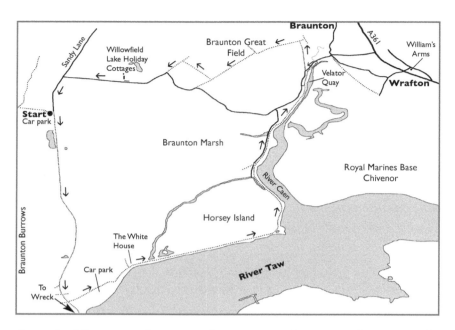

the end of the car park you reach a two-way fingerpost. Keep straight along the track. This is the South West Coast Path which here runs concurrent with the Tarka Trail, a footpath encompassing the area featured in Henry Williamson's book *Tarka the Otter*. You will occasionally see the logo of these two long distance paths: an acorn for the coast path and an otter's paw print for the Tarka trail.

Keep along the track, there is a lake with sand dunes beyond it to your right and occasional access through the fence into the area of the Burrows, which can be explored but are off the route of the walk. Follow the track for almost 1½ miles until you pass a three-way fingerpost indicating a bridleway off to the right, which you ignore. About 250m further you reach a two-way fingerpost (its badge denotes 'Boardwalk grid ref SS463328) indicating that the coast path now goes left along another track, but first you can divert to see the wreck.

For this diversion walk straight ahead from the fingerpost, passing a 'Christie Estates' information board advising that no naturist activities are permitted (amongst other things) followed by a row of large boulders.

You emerge through the dunes into the area of the Taw and Torridge estuaries known as Crow Point. Across the water lies West Appledore and nearer to hand you can see the colourful hull of a wrecked boat which is accessible if time and tide permit. Forlorn but atmospheric, he likes an occasional visitor and offers a good photo opportunity – before you set off towards the wreck take a note of your whereabouts so that you know where to head back to, to resume the walk.

Retrace your steps back from the wreck to the fingerpost to continue on the coast path as directed, the estuary now away to your right beyond the dunes. Keep ahead to reach Broadsands Car Park with its carved, wooden otter. Continue on the coast path along the track away from the car park until you reach The White House (shown as Crow Beach House on the OS map). Here, at the end of the track, you find more pointers taking you right, then very soon left, to circumnavigate the house. The coast path now follows a lovely raised route with the estuary to your right, the marsh and reed beds of Horsey Island to your left and the call of the curlew all around you. Across the water to your right are some rather striking jetties.

Wrecked boat at Crow Point

Looking back to The White House

Follow this raised path as it eventually swings left inland with the River Caen now to the right. A track, which becomes a tarmac lane, meets you from the left. Keep ahead and 1¾ miles from The White House you will find an old Toll House with its chickens down to the left. Stay on the path to cross a couple of stiles and keep going as before; away to your right you can see the Royal Marines Base of Chivenor. The path passes two signs proudly stating 'factory effluent discharge' and Velator Quay, where inhabited boats lie cheek by jowl with the odd wreck. Keep going on the coast path until you are confronted by the River Caen barring your way, at which point go left and up steps to join the lane at Velator Bridge on the edge of Braunton.

If you wish to head into Braunton for refreshments go right along the lane, otherwise turn left and follow the lane for about 150m until you find a track on the right between the houses of Riversview and Quay House. A footpath is signed along this track, follow it to a gate and in the field beyond keep ahead with the boundary on your right. After a second gate continue as before, at the time of writing new allotment gardens were being established in this field. At the end of the field leave through a gate and turn left to cross a stile, then walk through the field with the hedge to your left. The hedge soon ends and you find yourself walking through history as the path traverses the vast expanse of Braunton's mediæval Great Field.

The path follows the line of a slightly raised grassy headland and after 400m goes quickly right and left, as shown on a post, to continue as before across the field. A second post, after another 500m, gives you options. Follow the direction of the yellow arrow going right – you are heading towards the distant, pale building of the Saunton Sands Hotel. The path reaches the outside corner of a boundary. Keep ahead with the hedge on your left and at the end of the field a two-way fingerpost points you left along a track which brings you to a lane in 200m.

At the lane keep ahead to pass the Willowfield Lake Holiday Cottages in just under 500m. You reach a T-junction, turn left and this brings you back to the car park from whence you started.

Feudal farming

Braunton's Great Field is the remnant of a farming system dating back to mediæval times. Agricultural workers then owed varying degrees of allegiance and 'dues' to the lord of the manor. Some were freemen, whose ties were relatively minimal, but the class system was rife and below the freemen were the  lower social orders such as villeins and cottars. All had different amounts of land apportioned to them according to their status and this land was usually in huge, communal fields. From the Middle Ages Braunton's Great Field was organised in 'strips', each worker tilling a variable quantity of strips according to his or her rank. The field today is smaller than it once was and is now farmed by fewer people but the attractive patchwork of crops is redolent of the former strip system. Imagine the scene here centuries ago.... The modern OS map shows some of the field names. From the air the strips are still visible.

The reed-fringed marshes of Horsey Island make a great habitat for birds

Modern-day farming in Braunton's mediæval Great Field

Combe Martin & the Hangman Hills
Distance: 5 miles / 8km

This is a walk of fabulous contrasts, from the airy heights of the most lofty sea cliff in England, towering above the Exmoor coast, to an idyllic, fern-fringed, stream-side path, rich with wild flowers. Depending on the time of year this path can be glorious with primroses, wild garlic and the flowers of dog's mercury – a plant indicating ancient woodland. An easy-to-follow route but be prepared for a long ascent to start with – the views are worth the effort and benches offer respite. It's downhill all the way back. There is a very good chance of seeing Exmoor ponies (see feature on West Anstey Common walk), seals and maybe even a dolphin. Beautiful Herdwick sheep may be seen grazing en route.

Map: Outdoor Leisure 9, Exmoor 1:25 000

Start point: Kiln Car Park, Cross St, Combe Martin. Grid ref: SS577472, Postcode: EX34 0DH

Directions to start: Combe Martin is on the A399 five miles east of Ilfracombe

Parking: Kiln Car Park, Cross St, Combe Martin EX34 0DH

Public Transport: Bus companies that run through Combe Martin are Stagecoach and Filers Travel. Timetables available online at www.travelinesw.com. Nearest railway station is Barnstaple (8.8 miles)

Distance: 5 miles

Refreshments: Galleon Tea Room, Borough Rd, Combe Martin, 01271 883732; Quackers Restaurant at Ye Olde George and Dragon, Castle St, Combe Martin, 01271 882282

Toilets: At Kiln Car Park

Nearby places to stay: Blair Lodge, Moory Meadow, Combe Martin, 01271 882294; Poplars Hotel, Woodlands, Combe Martin, 01271 882240

Nearby places of interest: Chambercombe Manor, Chambercombe Lane, Ilfracombe, 01271 862624; Combe Martin Museum, Cross Street, 01271 889031; Combe Martin Wildlife and Dinosaur Park, 01271 882486

Possible birds include: Blackbird, blue tit, bullfinch, buzzard, carrion crow, chaffinch, dunnock, fulmar, goldfinch, house sparrow, jackdaw, gulls of various type, raven, robin, rook, shag, skylark, woodpigeon

Authors' tip: Combe Martin has a variety of annual events, ranging from the Strawberry Fair to the unique 'Hunting of the Earl of Rone'. Visit their website to see if you can coincide your visit with one of these festivals http://www.visitcombemartin.com/events-4/

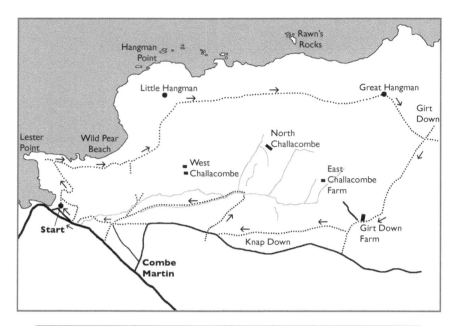

Note: **Be aware: part of the route is across open moorland, so a map and compass are necessary – and clear conditions. If you have a GPS it will be helpful**

Walk up the car park away from the public toilets and, just before entering the higher part of the car park, you will find access out onto the lane. A wooden sign by a telegraph pole indicates the acorn-waymarked coast path towards Lester Cliff and the Hangman Hills. This is your way, so leave the car park and follow the lane uphill, entering the Exmoor National Park. In a very short distance a fingerpost directs you right and in about 30m a further fingerpost points you off the tarmac lane and along a hedged track. In another 30m the coast path goes right off the track and up steps. Go with it.

This is a narrow path which climbs to meet a National Trust sign denoting the area of Little Hangman. Turn right and keep going, the sea is to your left as you approach the bulk of this smaller of the Hangman Hills. The coast path here runs concurrently with the Tarka Trail, a long distance path taking in the countryside featured in Henry Williamson's book *Tarka the Otter*.

Keep ahead on the coast path all the way to Little Hangman, ignoring a footpath going inland back to the village, another heading left to Wild Pear Beach (unless you want to visit it) and another heading right to West Challacombe Farm. Your way keeps going generally up to eventually skirt the peak of Little Hangman to your left, over 1 mile from the start of the walk. From here look ahead to where, 100m higher than his little brother, you can see Great Hangman, almost 1 mile away and the highest sea cliff in England. Don't be too deterred by this height, the bulk of the climbing is behind you and the ascent from here is less arduous. At one point the path goes right up steps and through a gate before continuing in the same direction. Keep with it all the way to the cairn on top of Great Hangman. A wonderful spot.

From here continue on the clear coast path which descends to the outside corner of a wall in 450m. This area is Girt Down and by the wall you find a three-way fingerpost. Leave the coast path here and go right towards the County Road. You now have lovely inland views to your left over the wall and, although you can't see the cairn, Great Hangman is up to your

The Exmoor Coast starts (or finishes) at Combe Martin

The Hangman Hills

Great Hangman, at 318m above sea level, is the highest sea cliff in England; Little Hangman is 218m. The origin of their curious names is a matter for conjecture. There is a possibility that a gallows once stood at the summit although it seems rather exposed for this. A more fanciful story tells of a sheep rustler  who was accidentally throttled by his own rope as he tried to steal sheep. A more likely explanation is that the name derives from the Celtic words 'au muen' meaning stone or rock. Great Hangman was used as a setting in the Leslie Charteris novel, *Meet the Tiger*, which featured Simon Templar as 'The Saint'.

right. This path leads to a stile, cross it and continue in the same line. A yellow-blobbed gate at the end of the next field leads to a track, still going in the same direction. Follow this when it swings right, ignore the agricultural debris, and you eventually pass Girt Down Farmhouse on your right. Beyond its gate you see a fingerpost, now follow the yellow-marked footpath ahead for Combe Martin.

Enjoy the lovely views across the valley to your right here, redolent of a Swiss scene and reminding us that the nearby area of Lynton and Lynmouth is referred to as 'Little Switzerland'. Within 150m of Girt Down Farm you find a footpath going right signed for Combe Martin via Knap Down Lane. Take this, there are more beautiful views to your right towards Little Hangman. This path continues for over ½ mile to reach a lane. Go right down the lane for less than 100m and you will find another footpath on the right, signed for Combe Martin in 1 mile. Take this broad track, descending to bend left across a stream in about 400m. Just beyond is a three-way fingerpost. Go left here over a stile, heading for Combe Martin via Hams Lane. This lush stretch of the walk beside the stream is quite idyllic. The obvious path crosses occasional plank bridges, always heading in the same direction until it emerges at a tarmac lane, which you follow in the same direction as before, between houses.

View to Little Hangman and the coast beyond

Towards Great Hangman

Waterfall on latter stage of walk

You reach a five-way fingerpost in about 100m. Fork right off the lane on the narrow path signed for 'beach via Hangman path'. (Don't take the sharp right path to Little Hangman.) Your way soon passes under a small footbridge and emerges in about 150m to cross a stream by the interesting-looking house of The Old Forge. Turn left here along the lane, passing the pre-school on the right. Keep on this lane as it bends left between houses and reaches the main road in Combe Martin at the junction of King Street and Borough Road. Turn right along the road, soon forking right down Cross Street towards the tourist information centre and the toilets. This leads back to Kiln Car Park.

Little Hangman from Knap Down

Walk 4

West Anstey Common

Distance: 5¼ miles / 8½km

This high, airy walk on the southern fringes of Exmoor offers some superb, view-rich moorland walking as well as an idyllic stretch through a verdant combe (or valley to the Exmoor-uninitiated!). You are very likely to see Exmoor ponies, possibly red deer and maybe the occasional small furry – a scuttling vole crossed our path. The walk is largely on tracks across access land and can be very wet underfoot after rain.

Map: Outdoor Leisure 9, Exmoor 1:25 000

Start point: Anstey Gate. Grid ref: SS835297

Directions to start: Anstey Gate is on the Ridge Road north of the Anstey villages and Molland. It can be accessed off the B3227

Parking: Anstey Gate, pull in areas off the Ridge Road

Public Transport: None

Distance: 5¼ miles

Refreshments: None en route but nearby is The London Inn, Molland, 01769 550269

Toilets: Gorse bushes!

Nearby places to stay: Ridler's Park, 01398 341213; Threadneedle Cottage, 01398 341213

Nearby places of interest: Exmoor Pony Centre, Ashwick, Dulverton, 01398 323093; Quince Honey Farm, 01769 572401

Possible birds include: Carrion crow, chaffinch, goldfinch, magpie, pheasant, raven, rook, skylark, starling, woodpigeon

Authors' tip: Wander along Ridge Road to the Memorial Stone, situated between Anstey Gate and the point further east where you cross the Ridge Road. An easy stroll amongst glorious views

Note: Be aware: part of the route is across open moorland, so a map and compass are necessary – and clear conditions. If you have a GPS it will be helpful, although some tracks used aren't shown on the OS map

---

At Anstey Gate you will find a fingerpost near the cattle grid. The path you need is the bridleway (not the footpath) signed for Hawkridge, which heads slightly north of east across the moorland. Depending on the ground conditions, you may notice two tracks heading in this direction, diagonally away from the road and the gate – the one you need is the further from the road and is well-trodden.

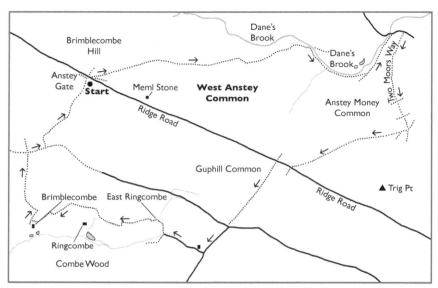

The bridleway goes gently downhill and you will find yourself heading towards a wooded combe. About 700m from Anstey Gate the path passes a dense thicket of gorse at grid ref SS841298 and continues downhill into the combe. At the bottom you reach Dane's Brook and a three-way fingerpost. This is a lovely spot, though the brook, which here is the boundary between Devon and Somerset, can be swollen after heavy rain. Don't cross the ford here, instead stay in Devon and turn right, following the permitted path towards Slade Bridge, the water down to your left.

Your way now follows the line of the brook on the permitted path, crossing an occasional tributary (these may dry up in summer) until you reach the lane just above Slade Bridge, almost 1km from the ford. Turn right up the lane and within about 150m you will spot a wooden post on the right opposite a farm gate. A white 'M' above 'W' denotes the Two Moors Way, you now follow this path right off the lane, climbing steadily. As you rise there are expansive views to your right, across the combe and into Somerset. Spare a glance behind you, the lane snakes up the valley with farms to left and right and a stone barn beside the lane.

Follow the Two Moors Way as it climbs, ignoring occasional crossing paths (at grid refs SS858296 and SS858295 – although these tracks are clear on the ground they are missing from the OS map!). Continue up towards a tree-topped boundary. When you reach it there is a three-way fingerpost by a broad crossing track. Two right hand options are shown, to West Anstey and to Yeo Mill. The Yeo Mill option is the one you need, so go right on the broad track and in about 15m fork right – this track now takes you westward across the amusingly-named Anstey Money Common. Keep ahead now on this broad, well-trodden path, ignoring any forks left or right and with lovely valley views to your right. The westerly direction swings slightly south of west, the valley still to the right. Behind to your right you can see the village of Hawkridge with its church tower.

Ignore any crossing paths, keeping ahead in the same direction until you reach the Ridge Road which leads to Anstey Gate. A bridleway continues opposite but ignore this and turn right along the road for 120m. Here you find a two-way fingerpost. If you've had enough keep going on the road back to your car at Anstey Gate. Otherwise, go left on the bridleway towards Yeo Mill, heading south west. The path drops downhill towards the right hand end of a line of conifers. When you get there cross the road,

Across the moor towards Dane's Brook

Fingerpost at Dane's Brook

passing a grassy triangle, and crossing a cattle grid to follow the lane towards Yeo Mill (as shown on the road sign).

Just over 250m along the lane you reach a right turn. Take this, it leads to a two-way fingerpost. Go right on the bridleway, passing the attractive East Ringcombe Cottage and walking between the house and the stables (respect their privacy please). At the end of the stables go through the gate and turn left on the blue-arrowed bridleway, keeping the field boundary to your left.

You reach another gate beyond which turn right to follow the boundary round the field as indicated by arrows, until you find a gate on the far side with another blue arrow. Go through two gates in quick succession then keep ahead through the next field, boundary to your left. When you reach a gate on the left with a yellow footpath arrow ignore it, staying in the same field and still following the blue bridleway arrow, boundary on your left. Notice the lichen-covered twigs in this boundary – a sign of clean air. At the end of the field an arrowed gate leads you out, the arrow directing you right uphill. Follow this, the line crosses a tarmac drive and ascends to another gate. This part of the bridleway has been officially diverted.

Follow the arrow's direction through the next field, boundary to your right, views to your left across the farm with the wooded hillside beyond. At the end of this field veer left across the next as directed, you can see the buildings of Brimblecombe ahead. When you reach the far side of the field an arrow directs you downhill beside the fence. You swiftly reach another gate, continue down the next field following the left hand boundary to the bottom corner. This ends in a steep descent to a bridleway gate straddling a stream. Go through and cross the next field in the direction of the arrow, stream to your left and rising ground to your right.

You meet a fence near the farm buildings, turn right along it and then quickly left round the outbuildings to another small gate. Beyond here bear right up the slope behind the buildings to emerge through another gate onto a partly-concreted track. Turn right up this and follow it as it bends left and leads up to a gate. Follow the clear track beyond and at

Exmoor ponies

The pure-bred Exmoor, recorded in the Domesday Book, is Britain's oldest native breed and has its own Society, founded in 1921, to help preserve the genetic integrity. They are bay in colour with lighter 'mealy' patches round muzzle and eyes, which are slightly prominent and 'hooded' to help  protect against rain. These attractive ponies are hardy and well-suited to living in exposed moorland conditions. During WWII they were used by troops for target practise and were also slaughtered for human consumption, which pressures almost resulted in their extinction. The population has, thankfully, recovered and is hugely popular as a riding pony. The grazing of the semi-feral ponies helps manage the moorland. Please don't offer the ponies titbits. It encourages them to approach people and cars which isn't good for their well-being.

the top of the field continue uphill with the track through another field to emerge through a gate beside a cattle grid. Open moorland is now ahead of you. Here you find a four-way fingerpost, go right on the clear bridleway towards West Anstey. In 150m take a left turn and follow this track back up to Anstey Gate and your start point.

Exmoor pony

Brimblecombe

The Hunters Inn, Woody Bay & Heddon's Mouth
Distance: 7.3 miles / 11¾km

The Exmoor coastline offers some of the best walking in the country and this route doesn't disappoint. It has the added advantage of a 360° viewpoint from a Roman Fortlet and you may see red deer in the woodlands around the valley. The paths are very easy to follow and although there are inevitable ascents and descents they are long and steady rather than challengingly steep. The Hunters Inn is an excellent port of call before and/or afterwards.

Map: OS Outdoor Leisure 9, Exmoor 1:25 000

Start point: The Hunters Inn. Grid ref: SS655480. Postcode: EX31 4PY

Directions to start: The Hunters Inn is halfway between Combe Martin and Lynton and is signed from the A39 at Killington Cross (grid ref: SS672456)

Parking: National Trust car park near the The Hunters Inn

Public Transport: None. Nearest railway station is Barnstaple (12 miles)

Distance: 7.3 miles

Refreshments: The Hunters Inn, 01598 763230

Toilets: Next to the National Trust Shop in the Heddon Valley

Nearby places to stay: Heddon's Gate Hotel, 01598 763481; The Hunters Inn, 01598 763230: Old Rectory Hotel, Martinhoe, 01598 763368; Woody Bay Hotel, 01598 763264

Nearby places of interest: Arlington Court (National Trust), Arlington, 01271 850296; Lynton & Barnstaple Railway, Parracombe, 01598 763487

Possible birds include: Blackbird, blue tit, buzzard, carrion crow, chaffinch, chiffchaff, dipper, dunnock, fulmar, goldcrest, great tit, green woodpecker, grey wagtail, guillemot, gulls of various type, house sparrow, long-tailed tit, peregrine, pied flycatcher, raven, razorbill, robin, skylark, song thrush, stonechat, whitethroat, willow warbler, wood warbler, woodpigeon, wren

Authors' tip: Look out for a variety of mammals. In this area we have seen foxes, deer and even a dolphin

From the inn take the lane going uphill to Martinhoe. As it bends right in a few metres go ahead off the lane, passing the roof of the inn (spot the jolly sunflower on the ridge) along a broad track shown as a bridleway to Heddon's Mouth and a footpath to Woody Bay, 2¾ miles away. Soon the bridleway forks left downhill and here you keep ahead on the footpath. This gently rising path winds up through the trees, high above the River Heddon down to your left, and eventually gives you good

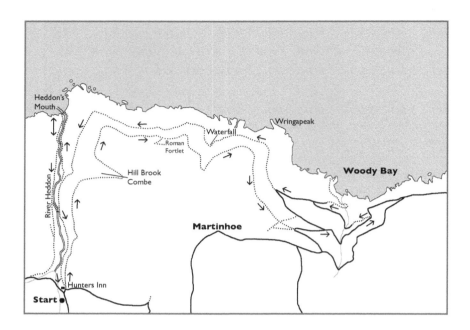

views out towards Heddon's Mouth before swinging right to head away from the Heddon Valley. The path now skirts the smaller valley of Hill Brook, keep going as it levels out and brings you round to the coast, the sea to your left, occasional benches to offer support and, as you proceed, grand views along the coast towards the furthest headland of Foreland Point with its winking lighthouse (see Lynmouth, Watersmeet and Countisbury walk). This high path is not the South West Coast Path, which is below you down the cliff.

You reach a fingerpost on your right directing you up to the Roman fortlet. We would recommend this extra climb for the stunning view when you get there – but it must have been a chilly place for soldiers used to Italy. From the top you can see Great and Little Hangman beyond the Heddon Valley (see Combe Martin walk) and there are also wonderful inland views. Descend from the fortlet and keep on along the footpath enjoying the coastal scenery and following it all the way to the woodland of Woody Bay. Depending on the degree of foliage you may get glimpses across the bay towards lovely houses set on the cliffsides.

When you reach the lane turn left downhill, passing a wide parking area on the right and ignoring a turning on the left. Keep on the lane as it descends and bends left over a beautifully mossy, stone bridge with a waterfall on the right – this may diminish in dry weather. You pass the rather grand building of a former hotel on the right and just beyond this go through the gate on the left to join the acorn waymarked coast path to Heddon's Mouth, 2½ miles away.

Follow the path through the woods until it emerges at the delightful 'Cottage at Trees', rather redolent of Hansel and Gretel. Beyond is a large fingerpost telling you which way to go for New Zealand, Russia, Iceland and America. If none of these take your fancy look for the more conventional three-way fingerpost and go left along the lane shown as a public footpath to Heddon's Mouth. Pass Hawks Hill Cottage and Oak Cottage, both on the right, and keep ascending with the lane until, at a sharp left bend, you find a footpath going right signed as the coast path to The Hunters Inn. Take this, ignoring a right fork in about 20m and climbing with the coast path as it leaves Woody Bay. You soon reach a

Early view of Exmoor coastline from above Heddon's Mouth

Views across Woody Bay to Lee Abbey

Icy falls alongside flowing water

Looking east from coast path

bench with fabulous views across glorious gardens with the bay and coastal headlands beyond. You can see the cream-coloured building of Lee Abbey above Lee Bay (see Valley of Rocks walk). Inland from this you can make out the start of the Valley of Rocks running parallel to the coast. Beyond Lee Abbey you will glimpse the Foreland Point lighthouse.

From the bench keep along the coast path as it goes under windswept trees, bowing over the path. Eventually you will hear, and then see, a waterfall; one cold February we found this partially frozen, the central section running but the side-falls frozen into shards of ice. It was one of the loveliest sights we have encountered. The path beyond here is quite close to the edge – watch your step and your dogs – although you are still well above the sea.

You arrive at Heddon's Mouth, a superb view and a place for peregrines. You can see the old lime kiln behind the beach. Follow the path as it goes left, gently descending into the valley to eventually land you beside the river at a three-way fingerpost. Go right on the bridleway towards the beach, a lovely stretch of riverside walking. When you reach the footbridge cross the river (the stepping stones further on are often submerged) and continue along the river to reach Heddon's Mouth.

The Hunters Inn

The original thatched cottage on this site was burned down at the end of the 19thC and rebuilt in a Swiss chalet style to reflect the favoured style in nearby Lynmouth and Lynton – also known as 'Little Switzerland'. The inn has, over the decades, been the haunt of the glamorous and well-known as well as more  regular folk. Not least amongst these is the granny of one of the authors. James Clancy's grandmother, Winifred Paul, visited this inn during the 1930s, and she's still here. A photograph of Winifred, pictured alongside some not-then vintage cars, is usually hanging on the wall of the bar. The inn was North Devon CAMRA Pub of the Year 2009.

After the beach return to the bridge and continue with the river on your left for about 500m until you find a three-way fingerpost. Here the coast path to Combe Martin goes ahead but the left option, going towards the river, is also coast path and this is your way, so fork left down steps towards the river. You pass through a gate, walking beside the river and soon cross a small, stone bridge. Turn right after it, keeping the river to your right and ignoring any left options. You reach a gate into the gardens of The Hunters Inn – and if this is your destination pass through and go in. If you're not planning a visit (which we would find surprising, quite frankly) bear left up the track to skirt the gardens, rising to join the footpath and lane along which you passed earlier and retracing your steps back to your car.

Spectacular Heddon's Mouth

Parracombe

This attractive, inland route offers a variety of terrain, wonderful views and good bird watching. The paths are clear though may be muddy in places. There is one long, steep section out of the Heddon Valley.

Map: Outdoor Leisure 9, Exmoor 1:25 000

Start point: Car park at top of village above Bodley Cross. Grid ref: SS670450. Postcode: EX31 4QL

Directions to start: Parracombe is signposted off the A39 between Lynton and Arlington

Parking: Car park at start point above

Public Transport: The number 309 and 310 buses pass through Parracombe and both are operated by Filers Travel. Timetables available online at www.travelinesw.com. Nearest railway station is Barnstaple (10.3 miles)

Distance: 6 miles

Refreshments: The Fox and Goose, 01598 763239; The Hunters Inn, 01598 763230

Toilets: In the car park

Nearby places to stay: The Fox and Goose, 01598 763239; Moorlands, Woody Bay, Parracombe, 01598 763224

Nearby places of interest: Arlington Court and the National Trust Carriage Museum (NT), 01271 850296; Exmoor Zoological Park, South Stowford, Bratton Fleming, 01598 763352; Lynton & Barnstaple Railway, Woody Bay Station, Martinhoe Cross, Parracombe, 01598 763487

Possible birds include: Blackbird, buzzard, carrion crow, chaffinch, chiffchaff, collared dove, dipper, dunnock, fieldfare, green woodpecker, grey wagtail, goldfinch, gulls of various type, long-tailed tit, pied wagtail, raven, siskin, skylark, whitethroat, willow warbler, woodpigeon, wren

Authors' tip: Nearby Heddon Hall opens its beautiful gardens during the summer so if this appeals you could time your visit to suit, 01598 763541

Leave the car park and turn left down the lane to reach Bodley Cross. Turn right towards Bodley and keep on the lane for 400m until it bends right, where you find a three-way fingerpost by West Bodley Farm which often has free range eggs for sale. Keep ahead on the bridleway 'via Newberry Lane'. This climbs and bends to another three-way fingerpost and your way lies through the gate and ahead to West Hill – good views as you walk through here with the boundary to your left. At the end of

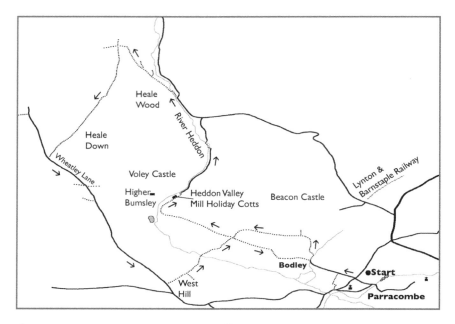

the field pass through a blue-blobbed gate and continue through the next field, boundary to your left.

At the end of this second field go through the gate and head down diagonally left to a gate with an adjacent fingerpost. Pass through and walk down the field with the boundary to your left. At the bottom of the field is a four-way fingerpost. Remember this spot as you'll be back here later. Your way now goes to the right, still in the same field, on a yellow-marked footpath with the boundary to your left. Go through the yellow-blobbed gate at the end of the field and continue as before, boundary still to the left. At the end of the field pass through into the next and continue as before, boundary to the left and the delightfully-named farm of Higher Bumsley in the valley ahead.

In the bottom corner of the field you find a two-way fingerpost directing you down the track beyond. From here there is an attractive view to the rising land of Voley Castle above and behind Higher Bumsley and you will see the River Heddon down to your left. The track descends to meet a broad track – keep ahead here along this track, passing the buildings of

Heddon Valley Mill holiday cottages on the left – this was previously known as Bumsley Mill but the name has been changed, which seems rather a shame. Keep going along the track passing a two-way fingerpost on the right until you eventually descend left to meet the entrance gates to the mill. Here a three-way fingerpost gives options – go right (effectively in the same direction as before) towards Heddon Valley, ½ mile away, following the tarmac drive.

In about 20m there is another fingerpost, continue on the tarmac drive – a lovely, easy stretch of walking beside the river. About 500m from the gates to the mill a fingerpost points you left off the drive across a footbridge into the woods. Follow this, going right at the end of the bridge and in a short distance the path crosses the river again to rejoin the drive and continue as before. This may seem an illogical detour but it's the way it's meant to be. The drive drops down to meet a lane, turn left along it and follow it for 350m until, opposite Mill Farm, you find a footpath ahead leading off the lane at a bend. (You may wish to follow the lane for ¾ mile to The Hunters Inn at this point, but return to Mill

Walking into the view

Iron Age Castles

Beacon and Voley Castles (latter pictured right) are two Iron Age hill forts, reminders of people long-gone who occupied this area. Such hill forts were our ancestors' refuges, occupying high ground for ease of protection against would-be attackers. Some hill forts were also used as trading posts or places for  social gatherings or 'moots'. The Iron Age was so called as by then iron had become the material of choice for tools and weapons. The period extended from, approximately, the 8thC BC to the 1stC AD. It was preceded by the Bronze Age which superseded the Stone Age, although the demarcation between the times was blurred and varied according to location.

Farm afterwards.) Arrows direct you diagonally left across the field to reach a footbridge. Cross and go right to keep the River Heddon to your right. Take a few deep breaths as it gets steep after this.

Follow the path as it ascends for 700 breathy metres. The lovely beech tree boundary on your right may help take your mind off the problem. Twice you meet three-way fingerposts but on both occasions you must summon up all your powers of abstemious rectitude and ignore the right pointer for The Hunters Inn (unless you are inclined to climb back up to this point afterwards). Your way lies skyward towards Trentishoe and Heale – and eventually you reach a gate and a mercifully flat patch.

Go through the gate and turn left, ignoring the gate you reach in about 30m and climbing (sorry) beside the left boundary and away from the trees for 70m to another gate with a yellow marker up in the corner of the field. Beyond this turn immediately left through yet another gate and walk straight across the field in an almost southerly direction, a fringe of trees over to your left. Pause a moment to look directly behind as you cross, there are very good views towards the coast at Heddon's Mouth (see Hunters Inn, Woody Bay & Heddon's Mouth walk). At the end of the first field continue through a second in the same direction to a gate in the far boundary, enjoying views to the left as well as behind. At the end of the second field continue as before into a third, now beside the boundary on the right, to then enter a fourth field. Half way through this the boundary bends slightly and you are joined by a track coming in from the right. Keep ahead on this track as it takes you into a fifth field, still going in the same direction. At the end go through a gate and continue as before through the sixth field. As you traverse this look right through gateways back to the headlands along the coast. The further and higher of the two huge hills you can see to the north west is Great Hangman with its cairn, the highest sea cliff in England (see Combe Martin walk). At the end of this field continue in the same direction through a seventh and after this you reach Wheatley Lane. Turn left.

You now follow this lane for just over 1 mile, enjoying its views and ignoring crossing footpaths after 400m and another on the right after a further 180m near West Middleton Farm, which goes to Voley Farm (not the same place as the hill fort). After 1 mile you reach a bridleway on the left to Parracombe. Take this, following the clear track downhill with a good view ahead towards Beacon Castle. Pass the entrance to West Hill

River Heddon

and keep going on the concrete track until it crosses the river, after which you see a two-way fingerpost still marking the bridleway. Veer right after the river, off the track and through a gate set at about 45° to the track, bearing a 'please shut the gate' sign and with 'ENP' carved into its framework – make sure you get the correct gate. Beyond it look out for the old, rather ornate bedstead in the right hand boundary and climb up the grassy slope to approach a cottage right against the path – please respect their privacy.

Beyond the cottage pass through the blue-marked gate and follow the narrow path, rising and bending through occasional muddy patches. You reach a four-way fingerpost which you've seen before. Go right through the gate to now follow the yellow-marked footpath with the boundary to the right – you are now walking the fourth and final arm of this meeting of ways. At the end of the field continue on the narrow path in the same direction. It bends right and descends, giving a nice view ahead to the village. You wind down to meet the lane at West Bodley Farm. Turn right to retrace your steps back to Bodley Cross and then left back up the lane to the car park.

Mossy creature in beech boundary   *The track beyond West Hill*

Valley of Rocks
Distance: 3½ miles / 5.6km

The natural geology of this location is an astonishing sight for first-time visitors. Add to this the outstanding scenery of the Exmoor coast, the appeal of the semi-feral goats (and their delightful kids at the right time of year) and the beautiful buildings of Lee Abbey and you have an exceptional, short walk. There are a couple of steep ascents but the paths are good and clear throughout.

Map: OS Outdoor Leisure 9, Exmoor 1:25 000

Start point: Valley of Rocks Car Park. Grid ref: SS711496. Postcode: EX35 6JH

Directions to start: Valley of Rocks can be easily reached from Lynton

Parking: Car park opposite cricket pitch

Public Transport: Nearby Lynton is served by buses from Filers Travel and Quantock Motor Services. Timetables available online at www.travelinesw.com. Nearest railway station is Barnstaple (14½ miles)

Distance: 3½ miles

Refreshments: Mother Meldrum's Tea Rooms & Garden, Valley of Rocks, 01598 753667; The Oak Room, Lee Road, Lynton, 01598 753838; Lee Abbey Tea Cottage, Lee Abbey, 01598 752621

Toilets: By the entrance to the car park

Nearby places to stay: Crown Hotel, Sinai, Lynton, 01598 752253; Lorna Doone House, 4 Tors Rd, Lynmouth, 01598 753354; Waterloo House, Lydiate Lane, Lynton, 01598 752575

Nearby places of interest: Exmoor Coast Boat Trips, 01598 753207; Glen Lyn Gorge, Lynmouth, 01598 753207; Lyn Model Railway, Watersmeet Road, Lynmouth, 01598 753330; Lynton & Lynmouth Cliff Railway, 01598 753486

Possible birds include: Blackbird, blue tit, carrion crow, chiffchaff, fulmar, guillemot, house martin, jackdaw, linnet, oystercatcher, pied flycatcher, pied wagtail, raven, razorbill, rook, song thrush, stonechat, willow warbler, wren

Authors' tip: For a real sense of achievement consider taking the perfectly negotiable path that winds its way to the summit of Castle Rock. Watch your step near the summit though as things begin to get a bit bouldery

Note: Be aware: part of the route is across high open land, so clear conditions are advisable

---

From the car park turn right up the lane towards a well-built shelter. Just before the cattle grid go left towards the shelter and a three-way fingerpost. From here follow the tarmac path signed for 'Lynton and Lynmouth via North Walk', you have good views over the cricket pitch

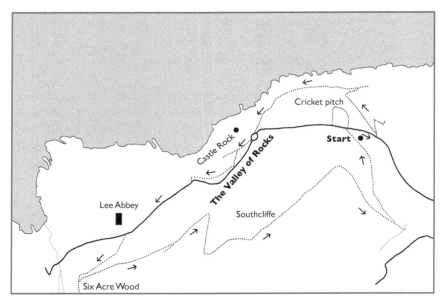

and of the valley. You soon reach the coast and the path bends right –
Foreland Point with its winking lighthouse is in the distance (see
Lynmouth, Watersmeet & Countisbury walk). The path drops down to
another three-way fingerpost by a little rocky shelter. Here go sharp left
to join the acorn waymarked coast path towards Castle Rock, the sea is
to your right, the views spectacular.

The path brings you past a telescope (the business end of which was
missing in action at the time of writing). Castle Rock towers up to your
right. Keep ahead as the tarmac path ends and you reach the lane near
the roundabout below Castle Rock. Turn right and walk along the lane –
if you prefer to keep off tarmac there is a grassy path to the right which
initially follows the line of the lane then drops away from it, later rising
to meet it again by the cattle grid and lodge to Lee Abbey. If you have
been following the grassy path, when you rejoin the road near the gates
to Lee Abbey turn left for about 100m back to a fingerpost indicating 'The
White Lady' – a curious rock formation that can be seen from this point.
If you're walking along the road you will have seen her on the way up.

Follow the lane from the cattle grid until you reach the mighty gatehouse
of the abbey on your right. Here go left off the lane to proceed along a

Admiring the Exmoor coastline from Castle Rock

Look out for goats both in the Valley of Rocks and along the coast path

broad track which is signed as a bridleway to Six Acre Cross and footpath to Lee Bay and Lynton. As you walk along this track glance back for a good view of the attractive main building of Lee Abbey. Lee Bay is down to your right. Follow the track for 350m until a broad track comes to meet you from the left near a two-way fingerpost. Go left up this track, the bridleway to Six Acre Cross, as it climbs through Six Acre Wood. The bridleway does a hairpin right after 600m, at which point keep straight ahead on the footpath for Lynton via Southcliffe. You soon go through a kissing gate, after which continue on the well-trodden path up the hillside, which is quite steep at times as it zigzags skywards. Eventually the path begins to level out and passes a gorse 'forest' on the right. You're very high here and as you continue the views are superb – this vantage point dwarfs the Valley of Rocks and you can see why Castle Rock is so named as from this aerial view it resembles the arrangement of a Norman castle.

The path starts to descend, below you can see your start point and anyone making an attempt on your car. Beyond another kissing gate the path soon enters trees and down to the left you will see the cemetery. Descend to meet an oblique crossing path and go left along it, still descending. Keep ahead past the cemetery. The path skirts the car park to reach the lane opposite the cricket pavilion. Go right along the lane to return to the car.

Looking down on Castle Rock from the heights of Southcliffe

Lee Abbey

Ascending Castle Rock

More goats

Valley of Rocks

This 'dry' valley, running parallel to the coast, is thought to have formed as a result of the East Lyn River flowing through it, although the course of this river has changed over time and it now meets the sea at Lynmouth. In the last Ice Age this area was at the very limit of glaciation and the spectacular, natural rock formations in the valley are the inspiration for many stories and legends. In R. D. Blackmore's *Lorna Doone* Mother Meldrum had her home here. Evidence of human settlement in the area dates back to the Bronze Age. Feral goats were recorded here in Domesday although the ancestors of the present herd were brought here from Northumberland in the 1970s. The goats are a hardy, native breed and their grazing, together with that of Exmoor ponies (see feature on West Anstey Common walk), helps to manage the land.

Walk 8

Lynmouth, Watersmeet & Countisbury

Distance: 5 or 7¾ miles / 8 or 12½km

Lynmouth is an attractive village with much history, some of which is encountered during the walk. This lovely route starts at sea level, exploring the wooded gorge of the River Lyn before climbing to lofty heights above the Exmoor coastline. The views are dramatic and varied, the paths good, but be prepared for ups, downs and edges – exercise caution near them. There are plenty of refreshment opportunities en route for refuelling. You have a very good chance of seeing red deer and Exmoor ponies plus excellent birdlife – around the Watersmeet Tea Gardens the wild birds are remarkably confiding.

Map: OS Outdoor Leisure 9, Exmoor 1:25 000

Start point: Road bridge in Lynmouth. Grid ref: SS723494. Postcode: EX35 6EX

Directions to start: Lynmouth is situated on the northern edge of Exmoor on the coast. It can be accessed via the A39

Parking: Lower Lyndale Car Park, Watersmeet Road, Lynmouth EX35 6ES

Public Transport: Lynmouth is served by buses from the following operators: Filers Travel and Quantock Motor Services. Timetables available online at www.travelinesw.com. Nearest railway station is Barnstaple (15 miles)

Distance: 5 or 7¾ miles

Refreshments: The Blue Ball Inn, Countisbury, 01598 741263; Rising Sun, Lynmouth Street, Lynmouth, 01598 753223; Watersmeet Tea Gardens (seasonal), 01598 753348

Toilets: Flood Memorial Hall and Lower Lyndale Car Park in Lynmouth. Plus Watersmeet (seasonal)

Nearby places to stay: The Blue Ball Inn, Countisbury, 01598 741263; Heatherville Hotel, Tors Park, Lynmouth, 01598 752327; Lorna Doone House, 4 Tors Rd, Lynmouth, 01598 753354; Waterloo House, Lydiate Lane, Lynton, 01598 752575

Nearby places of interest: Exmoor Coast Boat Trips, 01598 753207; Glen Lyn Gorge, Lynmouth, 01598 753207; Lyn Model Railway, Watersmeet Road, Lynmouth, 01598 753330; Lynton & Lynmouth Cliff Railway, 01598 753486

Possible birds include: Blackbird, blue tit, buzzard, carrion crow, chaffinch, dipper, grey wagtail, guillemot, gulls of various type, hawfinch, heron, great tit, jackdaw, linnet, mallard, oystercatcher, pied wagtail, raven, razorbill, robin, rook, shag, song thrush, stonechat, willow warbler, woodpigeon, wren

Authors' tip: The Foreland Point Lighthouse is now automated and the buildings converted into a wonderfully remote, National Trust holiday cottage. A

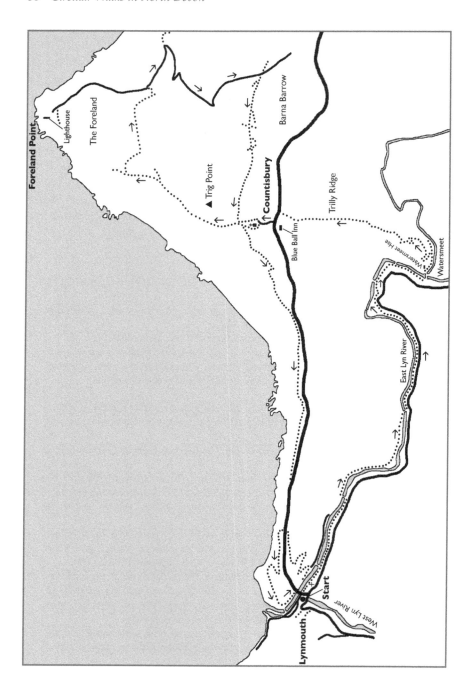

Foreland Point

Lighthouse

The Foreland

Trig Point

Barna Barrow

Countisbury

Trilly Ridge

Blue Ball Inn

Watersmeet Hse

Watersmeet

East Lyn River

West Lyn River

Lynmouth

Start

short detour brings you to a viewpoint from which you can see the light winking away and which affords glorious views eastwards along the coast

Note: **Be aware: part of the route is across open moorland, so a map and compass are necessary – and clear conditions. If you have a GPS it will be helpful**

From the main road over the river in Lynmouth descend steps to follow the path with the East Lyn River on your left, walking away from the coast and passing a car park on your right. Pass a footbridge in 200m without crossing and continue to the second bridge: before you reach it you will pass Middleham Memorial Gardens, site of cottages destroyed in the 1952 flood disaster. At the second bridge (Woodside Bridge) cross the river and now follow the frequent signs for Watersmeet, always taking the riverside option when there are choices and ignoring any signs for Countisbury for the time being – that comes later. This river is beautiful at all times of year and is spectacular after heavy rain. The route crosses the river again at Backpool Bridge after which you keep the river to your left. Keep going and the path eventually takes you past the site of the former Lynrock Mineral Water Factory, whose buildings were

Along the East Lyn River to Watersmeet

Watersmeet

Set at the confluence of the East Lyn River and Hoar Oak Water, this beautiful house was built as a 19thC fishing lodge and 'romantic retreat' by Rev Walter Halliday, lord of the nearby Manor of Glenthorne and great admirer of the poets Coleridge, Wordsworth and Shelley, who had likened the local scenery  to that of the Alps (which probably gave rise to the description 'Little Switzerland'). In 1901 Watersmeet became a refreshment stop serving teas, which happy situation continues to this day. The woodland tea gardens are a wonderful place to partake – although its more majestic trees have been lost in recent years. Excellent for birdlife, we once shared a table with a hawfinch. In this tranquil spot it's hard to imagine the nearby tragedy of the Lynmouth Flood Disaster of 1952 when 34 people were killed.

destroyed in the flood but where you can still see an old fireplace and one of the company's ginger beer bottles set into the right hand wall of the gorge. The path is up and down at times but follows the line of the river until it brings you to Watersmeet House, 1¾ miles from Lynmouth. A rustic post fence leads you down to cross Hoar Oak Water followed by the East Lyn River – the two waters that meet here.

After the bridges the walk goes right, passing Watersmeet House on your left with the river to your right. Beyond the house you find a fingerpost denoting the Fisherman's Path to Rockford and Brendon. Take this, climbing steeply to a three-way fingerpost where a left option points you towards Countisbury. This is now your direction so go left up steps, following the path as it winds up through the woodland – don't be tempted to veer off on any downhill options. The path eventually begins to level out and the trees become more sparse. The path forks, both options reconvening in a few metres at a four-way fingerpost about 700m from the river. Here you have two choices for Countisbury – take the yellow-marked one straight on (which is through a gate a little to the right of this post). The well-trodden path goes up the field beyond the gate, passing thickets of gorse and a lone post with a confirmatory arrow carved into it. Enjoy the views behind as you climb.

This line takes you across the delightfully-named area of Trilly Ridge, bringing you to the corner of the field and a series of gates. Keep straight on for Countisbury and you'll find yourself walking along a broad track between stone walls. Countisbury Church is ahead and slightly closer to hand you'll see The Blue Ball, a welcome stop for muddy boots and dogs. When you reach the road turn left along it (watch out for traffic) and in 85m go right along the lane signed for the church, unless you are diverting first for some succour at the inn.

Visit the church, which has Saxon origins, and notice the framed poster at the back advertising Countisbury's Coronation Festivities in June 1911, when King George V was crowned. From the church porch follow the path round to the back and leave the churchyard via the gate leading to access land on the headland. From here follow the well-trodden path going slightly right to find a four-way fingerpost at the stone wall with a bench beyond, within 100m of the church gate.

Waterfall, Watersmeet

Relic of Lynrock Mineral Water Factory

Now you have options. For those on the shorter route continue from (**) below. Otherwise, for the longer route, from the post follow the coast path option obliquely left. This path takes you away from the wall and onto the headland with the sea to your left and you will enjoy spectacular views westwards towards Lynmouth Harbour and beyond – as always exercise care near the edges. You reach a three-way fingerpost, keep on the coast path towards Porlock (you will occasionally see the white acorn symbol of the coast path on these signs). You reach another fingerpost in just over 200m with an onward finger pointing you to the Lighthouse – follow its direction, still on the marked coast path but heading slightly inland, passing the bulky 'rear' of Foreland Point to your left. The path begins to drop and below you see a surfaced track which leads to the lighthouse. As we descended to join this we had a wonderful view of three red deer stags watching us from across Coddow Combe.

When you reach the tarmac track go left if you wish to follow the Authors' Tip (p.49), otherwise turn right over the bridge and begin the long ascent uphill, a bit of a drag but easy underfoot. About 300m from

The long ascent uphill from Coddow Combe

The walk back to Lynmouth

the bridge the track swings right towards the county road, as shown on a fingerpost over to the left. Continue right, uphill on the tarmac leaving the coast path to carry on without you.

Just over ½ mile from the bend you reach a two-way fingerpost. Go right on the yellow-marked dirt track towards Countisbury, 1 mile away. Ahead of you in the distance you can see a mast. Ignore a right fork in roughly 40m but about 180m from the tarmac track there is a clear fork and here you take the right option, which is, in effect, straight on. Ignore left turns in 100m and again in another 50m. Keep ahead on the clear path, across another distinct crossing track, the mast now obliquely to your right, and you eventually reach another crossing track by a stone wall, 550m from leaving the tarmac track. Here turn right, following the line of the wall on your left with its occasional reassuring yellow blobs. As the track swings right yellow blobs on fence posts guide you to stay with the path beside the wall, leaving the track and walking between gorse bushes with the wall still to your left. You see the familiar buildings of Countisbury down to your left and you reach a bench and fingerpost which you should recognise from earlier.

(**) From the fingerpost leave the wall and follow the coast path with the sea to your right, passing the gate into the churchyard over on the left. You soon meet the wall again, keep it to your left and don't be tempted to cross it at any point as you follow the coast path down occasional steps on your way back to Lynmouth, about 1¾ miles away. The wall ends, keep going in the same direction, enjoying the views and eventually passing the remnants of disused quarry workings.

Lynmouth Harbour

Keep following the clearly-signed coast path until it brings you out to the road. Turn right along the road, walking through a lay-by area at the end of which a narrow earth path leads off beside the road. Follow this to keep out of the traffic for 280m to a three-way fingerpost, beyond which follow the acorn way-marked coast path away from the road and into the trees. This winds down and is clearly signed all the way, eventually landing you on a tarmac lane with a stone wall in front. Turn right then swiftly left, circumnavigating the buildings and gardens of The Manor House, which had some rather quirky artwork on display when we passed. Follow the broad, tarmac path round the environs of The Manor House, harbour to your right and Lynmouth's buildings ahead. The path winds back towards the river. Turn left beside it to return to the road bridge from which you started.

Mortehoe & Lee

Distance: 7¼ miles / 11½km

A superb walk encompassing some of the best coastal scenery on offer, verdant woodland, delightful villages and an excellent dog-friendly pub en route. The area is brilliant for bird watching – you have the chance of seeing peregrine, the fastest creatures on earth when they stoop. You may also see seals and possibly dolphins. Inevitably the walk involves some steep ups and downs but it really is worth the effort.

Map: Outdoor Leisure 139: Bideford, Ilfracombe & Barnstaple 1:25 000

Start point: Mortehoe Car Park. Grid ref: SS457452. Postcode: EX34 7DT

Directions to start: Mortehoe is 6 miles west of Ilfracombe and 1¼ miles north of Woolacombe

Parking: Mortehoe Car Park

Public Transport: The number 31 and 303 buses pass through Mortehoe and both are operated by Filers Travel. Timetables available online at www.travelinesw.com. Nearest railway station is Barnstaple (10 miles)

Distance: 7¼ miles

Refreshments: Chichester Arms, Mortehoe, 01271 870411; Grampus Inn, Lee, 01271 862906; Rockleigh House, The Square, Mortehoe, 01271 870704

Toilets: In Mortehoe Car Park and in Lee

Nearby places to stay: Rockleigh House, The Square, Mortehoe, 01271 870704; Shaftsboro Farm, Lee, 01271 865029

Nearby places of interest: Chambercombe Manor, Chambercombe Lane, Ilfracombe, 01271 862624; Mortehoe Museum, 01271 870028

Possible birds include: Blackbird, blue tit, buzzard, carrion crow, chaffinch, dunnock, fulmar, gannet, green woodpecker, guillemot, gulls of various type, jackdaw, kestrel, magpie, mallard, meadow pipit, oystercatcher, peregrine, raven, robin, sanderling, shag, stonechat, woodpigeon, wren

Authors' tip: If you like beaches consider a short journey to Woolacombe. It's one of the finest in the country and is renowned for its vast expanse of sand and excellent surf

Note: Be aware: part of the route is across open moorland, so a map and compass are necessary – and clear conditions. If you have a GPS it will be helpful

---

From the car park turn left along the lane through the village, towards the parish church. Just before the church, as the road swings left, go right

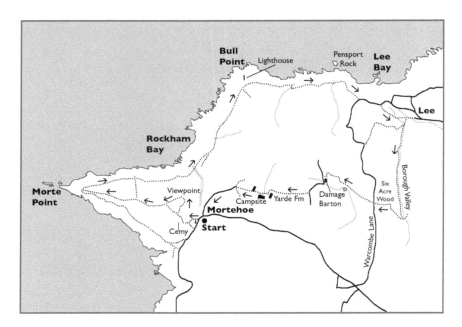

up the lane towards the village hall and cemetery, passing the church on your left and heading for the coast path. Keep straight ahead when you reach the cemetery, following a dirt track to pass through gates. This is Morte Point Memorial Park and is all access land. You will see an information board about the area not far from the gates. Near here you will also find a wooden fingerpost pointing you uphill to an elevated viewpoint.

Head for this viewpoint, winding your way up in the direction of the pointer to the top of the hill, about 300m away from the information board. The paths are well-trodden although there are only occasional arrows, but keep heading up until you find the site of the former lookout which was built at the start of WWI but demolished in 1932. The spot was well-chosen as the views are superb and the men who kept watch are commemorated on one of the plaques here: John Dyer, Thomas Parker and Samuel Yeo. Morte Point juts out into the sea to the west, north east of it along the coast is the lighthouse at Bull Point and looking south is the vast expanse of Morte Bay and Woolacombe Beach.

From here you can see the path out to the end of Morte Point. Descend from the lookout and walk west towards the point, a fabulous stretch of walking which abounds with some enticing paths – relish it. The route of the walk keeps heading west, dropping down towards the sea until, just above the end of the headland, you meet a clear, hard-trodden, earth crossing path, the South West Coast Path. At this point it is also the Tarka Trail, a long distance path crossing the countryside celebrated in Henry Williamson's book *Tarka the Otter*. Turn right along the coast path, the Atlantic to your left.

You now follow the coast path, passing Rockham Bay, all the way to the lighthouse at Bull Point, just under 2 rugged miles away. Ignore any footpaths heading inland back to Mortehoe, unless you're tiring and want an escape route – you will see the village outskirts as you continue. When you reach Bull Point Lighthouse look for the three-way fingerpost and continue on the coast path to Lee, 1½ miles away. Eventually you reach a footbridge spanning a stream – enjoy the lovely seaward view then keep going. It was near here that we had a good view of peregrine on the cliffs.

Walking towards Morte Point

Rugged coastal scenery

The coast path crosses a second footbridge some way on and when you reach a three-way fingerpost denoting 'steep path to sandy cove' to the left, ignore it unless you wish to explore. Your way continues up steps on the coast path above Lee Bay. This area is called Damage Cliffs. The path reaches a lane on the outskirts of Lee, turn left down it and follow it for about 300m as it swings right past the large gates of Lee Manor. A little way beyond here you find a right turn with a multiple-fingered post set against the wall. Leave the coast path, going right along this lane signed for the car park, toilets and footpath to Lee village.

Pass the car park on your left, followed by the public toilets. The tarmac lane becomes a stony path, keep ahead to reach a footpath fingerpost on the right. This is your way but first we strongly suggest you keep ahead into the village for a short detour to The Grampus Inn and a look round this attractive area, before returning to this fingerpost.

Back at the fingerpost cross the stile and walk through the field with the wall on your left. At the end of the field cross another stile followed by a footbridge into woodland with a nearby three-way fingerpost. Your route

Bull Point Lighthouse and Trinity House

The original Bull Point Lighthouse was built in 1879 after many ships succumbed off the coast here. In 1972 the headland subsided rendering some of the buildings unsafe. For two years Trinity House used an old lighthouse tower, imported from Braunton, while another lighthouse was constructed  further back from the cliff edge. Equipment from the old lighthouse was put to use in the new one. The foghorn ceased its call in 1988 and the lighthouse is now fully automated, its associated buildings finding a new lease of life as holiday cottages.

The corporation of Trinity House, whose remit is to aid the safety of shipping and seafarers, is a charity that received a Royal Charter from Henry VIII in 1514. This was granted to a fraternity of seafarers called The Guild of the Holy Trinity who regulated the pilotage of shipping in waters frequented by the King. Trinity House is best known for its administration of the lighthouse system of England, Wales, the Channel Islands and Gibraltar but also provides other aids to navigation such as lightships, buoys and satellite navigation. It also licences and supplies Deep Sea Pilots who assist ships with navigation, and another, less familiar aspect of its work is the provision of retirement homes for ex-mariners.

Lee Bay

follows the path beside the stream through the refreshing, sylvan area of Borough Valley. In just over ½ mile you reach a crossing path. When we were here a three-way fingerpost leant drunkenly against the bank. Left goes down to a footbridge but the way you want is, we're afraid, steeply uphill through the trees on the path to Damage Barton. Emerge from the woodland and cross the stile a short distance away, walking through the field beyond in the direction of the yellow arrow. You reach a stile, followed by a lane with a high stile on the far side. The post adjacent to this high stile was pointing in a rather misleading direction. From the stile look diagonally right across the field to glimpse another fingerpost in the distance, beyond the field corner and set high up. Follow this line to a gate set back in the corner and beyond this bear right up the bank to the elevated fingerpost.

From here the route varies slightly to what is shown on the OS map. Take the right hand option from the post which points across the field to an obvious gate in the far right hand boundary. When you get there you may spot a well-engorsed fingerpost to the right of the gate – it's hard to see it without lacerating your face. From the gate follow the track through

The coast path   Walking through Borough Valley

the field – the track is sometimes clear, sometimes indistinct. You may notice a pond beyond the fence to the left if you veer over. Keep going on the track as it winds between gorse bushes. You reach a two-way fingerpost 250m from the gate, which has both pointers going back! Keep ahead here to a yellow-topped post within 100m.

At this post go almost 90° left to descend past a few trees and gorse bushes to a well-concealed gate about 100m from the post. Through the gate you'll find another yellow-arrow directing you down to quickly meet a clear path along which you turn right. You are now approaching the farm buildings of Damage Barton. Within 50m you reach a clear track and a two-way fingerpost. Go left down the track and at the buildings turn right, still on the track with the wall of an old stone barn on your left. At the end of the wall you enter a yard area, bear diagonally left across the yard and you'll see a clear sign pointing you towards Mortehoe.

Follow this direction, passing the attractive house on your left and walking along the drive past a pond – an area beautiful with snowdrops in the early part of the year. Keep going up the drive, passing occasional benches, until, about 250m from the house, you find a footpath going right as the drive bends left. The yellow arrow points you through the field with the boundary to the right. At the end of the field you find two gateways. Go through the one on the left, continuing with the boundary still on your right. This rises to another gate, beyond which keep going in the same direction, boundary to your right.

At the end of the field cross the stile and descend the path beyond, down steps, to arrive at Yarde Farm. A two way fingerpost directs you ahead on the track to reach a three-way fingerpost in about 50m. Go through the gateway, walking diagonally left through the field, still towards Mortehoe. This brings you to the far bottom corner of the field. Go through a gate then follow the path past a pond. The path winds between buildings, follow the arrows to arrive at the business area of a camping and caravanning site. Keep ahead past the various facilities and away from the buildings, following the drive in a westerly direction to reach gates, emerging from the site onto a lane. Go left on the lane and follow it for about 0.3 mile, back to the centre of the village and the car park from which you started.

Walk 10
North Molton
Distance: 3 miles / 4.8km

An easy-to-follow walk through some delightful water meadows and offering glorious 'gate-way' views on the way back to the village. There is an uphill stretch on the way back.

Map: OS Explorer 127, South Molton & Chulmleigh 1:25 000
Start point: The Square, North Molton. Grid ref: SS736298. Postcode: EX36 3HP
Directions to start: North Molton is clearly signed off the A361 North Devon Link Road
Parking: In The Square, which is situated just below the church at the hub of the village
Public Transport: Bus operators that call at North Molton are: Stagecoach Devon, TT Coaches and Beacon Bus. Timetables available online at www.travelinesw.com. The nearest railway station is Umberleigh (8.9 miles)
Distance: 3 miles
Refreshments: Bulled's village shop for snacks, 01598 740232; The Miners Arms, 01598 740316; The Poltimore Inn, 01598 740338 (reopening after refurb)
Toilets: Adjacent to Victory Memorial Hall on Fore Street
Nearby places to stay: Sannacott, North Molton, 01598 740203; Zeales, North Molton, 01598 740356
Nearby places of interest: Castle Hill Gardens, Filleigh, 01598 760336; Quince Honey Farm, South Molton, 01769 572401; South Molton Museum, 01769 572951
Possible birds include: Blackbird, blue tit, buzzard, chaffinch, dipper, great tit, house martin, house sparrow, jackdaw, jay, pheasant, robin, swallow, swift, woodpigeon, wren
Authors' tip: The Grade I listed, All Saints' Church, towering above The Square, dates from 15thC and is worth a visit

From The Square walk down East Street, passing The Miners Arms and enjoying countryside views ahead. After about 500m you find a clearly signed footpath on the right. Follow this and soon the houses drop away. This deep path descends for 300m then swings sharply right, following the line of a stream. The path soon goes left to cross the water then continues uphill before levelling out to give lovely views to the left.

Keep going through occasional yellow-arrowed gates descending towards the River Mole and following the bottom fringe of woodland up

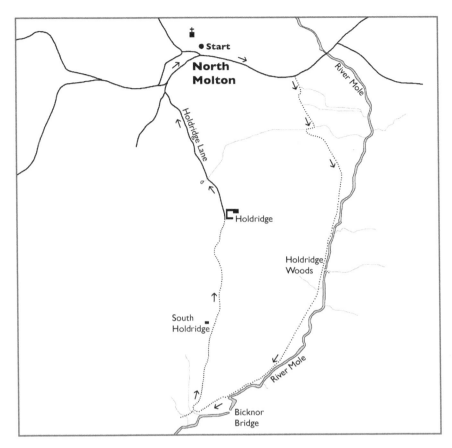

to your right – don't be tempted to veer off into it. The path brings you
down to the valley, the river over to your left across a water meadow.
Your way now follows the line of the river, which meanders in and out
to the left, the woodland still up to your right – a delightful stretch of
level walking. Pass through occasional gates and, after walking 500m
along the valley, you reach a small footbridge which carries a footpath
you don't need across the Mole. Ignore this bridge and keep going
beyond it for another 1km, river to your left. You pass through more
occasional gates until a fenced hedgebank stops you proceeding along
the river. Here a fingerpost about 50m to the right of the river, beside a
gate and below a conifer plantation, directs you out of the field and onto
a broad crossing track. The footpath continues on but you now leave it

View from Holdridge Lane

Early stages of the walk

Inquisitive sheep

Trees by River Mole

Mining round North Molton

The Miners Arms derives its name from the time when this area had many active mine workings. The earliest was The Bampfylde Mine, reputedly dating from the reign of King John (1199–1216), although it didn't take the name 'Bampfylde' until 1811 (see also feature on Yarde Down walk.) It had also variously been called the Copper Mine, The Prince Regent Mine and the Prince Albert Mine. From the Elizabethan era miners came here from as far afield as Germany. The industry was at its height during the 18thC–19thC and a

tramway transported ore from North Molton to the railway station at South Molton. The walk partly follows the route of this tramway near the river. Copper and iron were the principal ores but lead, silver and gold have also been found in the area – indeed specks of gold are still occasionally found. There are many mine remains around the area, all on private land. The only remaining mine building is a 'crusher house' which is being consolidated by a few members of the Exmoor Mines Research Group.

and turn right uphill on this unsigned track, heading away from the river. This is Holdridge Lane.

Although initially steep, the superb views across the valley from gateways make the effort worthwhile. The track eventually becomes well-surfaced and just under 2km from the river brings you back to North Molton. Turn right along the road towards the church tower, peeping over the rooves ahead of you. The road brings you back to The Square and your start point.

Brownsham & Clovelly
Distance: 6¼ miles / 10km

This glorious walk encompasses an Iron Age promontory hill fort, views to Lundy and across Bideford Bay, verdant woodland, a lovely stretch of undulating coastline, a rocky smugglers' beach and the chance to visit a unique village. The outward section of the route is rather harder walking than the return stretch on an inland bridleway. The route can be muddy after wet weather and rough underfoot at Mouth Mill. Birds are usually good, even on dull days.

Map: OS Explorer 126, Clovelly and Hartland 1:25 000

Start point: Brownsham Car Park (National Trust). Grid ref: SS285259. Postcode: EX39 6AN

Directions to start: Brownsham is between Hartland and Clovelly, accessed north off the B3248

Parking: Brownsham Car Park (National Trust)

Public Transport: Bus companies that operate in the Brownsham area are Stagecoach and Hemmings Coaches. Timetables available online at www.travelinesw.com. Nearest railway station is Barnstaple (17.2 miles)

Distance: 6¼ miles

Refreshments: Picnic spots en route and refreshments in Clovelly. Otherwise The Hart Inn, The Square, Hartland, 01237 441474

Toilets: At Clovelly Visitor Centre

Nearby places to stay: East Dyke Farmhouse B&B, Clovelly, 01237 431216; Fuchsia Cottage, Higher Clovelly, 01237 431398; Southdown Cottage B&B, Higher Clovelly, 01237 431504

Nearby places of interest: Clovelly village and Clovelly Court Gardens, 01237 431781; Hartland Abbey, Hartland, 01237 441234

Possible birds include: Blackbird, blackcap, blue tit, buzzard, fulmar, great tit, grey wagtail, gulls of various type, house sparrow, jackdaw, jay, magpie, pheasant, robin, shag, song thrush, starling, treecreeper, woodpigeon

Authors' tip: If you are planning to detour off the route and visit the Clovelly Visitor Centre and the village itself be aware that there is an entrance fee, payable in the Visitor Centre

---

At the back of the car park a fingerpost directs you along a track towards Beckland Woods and the coast path, one mile away. This leads to a gate entering woodland, just beyond which a fingerpost low down on the right points you downhill to cross a footbridge, heading for Windbury

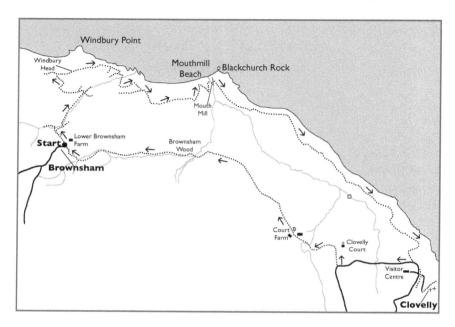

Hill Fort. At the far side of the bridge go right, still towards Windbury. The coast path here is signed as a mere ¼ mile, so you've just walked the quickest ¾ mile you're ever likely to. You now follow a lovely sylvan path, stream down to your right, to reach another three-way fingerpost beside a bridge. Don't cross the bridge but keep on for Windbury, swiftly reaching a few steps on the left which you climb, then heading left uphill through the woods. In about 150m another three-way post tells you to keep straight on for Windbury – obey it.

The path climbs and just before the end of the woodland it swings right to bring you to a gate into the environs of this Iron Age hill fort, the summit of which is 142m above sea level. Beyond the gate bear right to pick up the trodden path which winds up to the fort, keeping with the path as it climbs to eventually bring you to a three-way fingerpost above Beckland Cliff at grid ref SS284266. Here you go right on the acorn-waymarked coast path towards Mouth Mill two miles away, enjoying fabulous sea views and equally good ones inland. Ahead, at sea level on Mouthmill Beach, you will see Blackchurch Rock, which bears a strong resemblance to the old 'Monopoly' iron.

View to Blackchurch Rock

The Angel's Wings

Keep going on the coast path which eventually winds downhill back on itself – you are still following signs for Mouth Mill whenever you have an option. The path crosses Windbury Woods bridge at SS291265 then climbs steps and zigzags back up the cliff. On a gloomy day the gorse hereabouts can really brighten the darkness. The path descends towards Mouth Mill, entering woodland as you approach it and depositing you beside the ruined buildings, once a favoured haunt of smugglers. At low tide you can scramble out to Blackchurch Rock but watch the tides and don't get cut off.

Follow the coast path signs to cross the stream by Mouth Mill, then follow the clear track, climbing out of the valley and keeping an eye open for the two-way fingerpost about 450m from the stream that points you left off the track to continue with the coast path. Another pointer invites you to head for a viewpoint – if you accept this return to the coast path and keep going, watching your step near the edges. As you continue you pass the area of Gallantry Bower on the coast and have inland views across to Clovelly Court. The path enters woodland, keep watching for coast path signs and don't deviate inland.

You reach a delightfully-carved, Grade ll listed, wooden hut, The Angel's Wings, constructed in 1826 and restored in 1934, in memory of Marion Stucley. A beautiful spot for your picnic, enhanced for us by the presence of a tree-creeper who was having his 'sandwiches' nearby when we arrived. Keep going beyond The Angel's Wings, ignoring an inland path for the church and keeping on the coast path as it emerges from the woodland at some rather grand gates. You then re-enter woods and soon reach The Cabin, another picnic-stop.

Beyond this the path swings inland, enters a field and soon passes through a wrought-iron kissing gate, skirting the parkland and eventually reaching more grand gates to join the lane. Turn right uphill to meet a T-junction in a few metres. The walk continues to the right along the lane, but if you wish to visit Clovelly turn left, returning to this spot when you've finished exploring. Follow the lane, ignoring a left turn and beyond it keeping on the pavement until you reach the gates of Clovelly Court, 700m from the T-junction. Here a bridleway sign directs you right

Clovelly

Clovelly's human history probably dates back to the Iron Age or earlier with a settlement above today's village, the site of which was subsequently occupied by the Romans. More recently, from the time of Elizabeth I, the prosperity of the village was based on herring fishing. This declined in the early 19thC and tourism started to provide an income. Clovelly features frequently in literature, most notably that of Charles Kingsley who was the son of the rector. The popularity of his novels, *The Water Babies* and *Westward Ho!*, enticed people to visit. This privately-owned village has belonged to only 3 different families during the course of almost 800 years. In 1738 the Hamlyn family bought the estate for £9,438 and their descendants still own it today. The Clovelly Estate Company manages the village and its buildings, maintaining this characterful place to a high standard.

Miss Clovelly

down the drive. Take this, the verges can be pretty with flowers depending on the time of year. As you approach the buildings you will see the church on your right and a fingerpost pointing you left, still on the tarmac bridleway.

Follow this into woodlands and keep ahead, ignoring a pointer in about 200m back to the coast path and staying on the bridleway until you pass the buildings of Court Farm and Dairy Cottage. The tarmac finishes and the track becomes stony, keep ahead beyond the farm buildings looking for blue arrows to reassure you. You pass through a gateway where a blue arrow directs you to veer slightly right off the track, heading across the field towards woodland. This line brings you to an arrowed gate in the far hedge, continue beyond here down the next field with fenced woodland to your right. You reach the bottom corner of the field where, set down quite deeply in the corner, you find a gate entering woodland.

Beyond this follow the blue arrow along a stony track, heading downhill through a conifer plantation – which was being logged when we were there so we hope there's some left. The track descends for about 250m to meet a broader track. The fingerpost was supine when we passed, pointing at the sky, but your way lies to the left along this broad track to reach another fingerpost in just over 100m. Go right when you get there, crossing a stream and arriving at another junction of forestry tracks in less than 100m. Go left here and keep following the clear track through the woodland until you reach the lane at Lower Brownsham Farm just over 1km further on. Turn left up the lane away from the farm and a short way along on the right hand side you will find steps leading up to the car park from which you started.

Walk 12
Malmsmead & Brendon
Distance: 4½ miles / 7¼km

This lovely inland route has been a favourite of ours for many years. You will be unlucky not to see Exmoor ponies, you may see red deer and the deep valley views are superb. The riverside stretch of walking is delightful and offers good bird watching. There are some stout ascents but don't let this put you off, the paths are clear throughout.

Map: Outdoor Leisure 9, Exmoor 1:25 000

Start point: Lorna Doone Car Park, Malmsmead. Grid ref: SS791477. Postcode: EX36 6NU

Directions to start: Malmsmead is a hamlet situated 4.7 miles inland to the east of Lynton. It can be accessed along lanes from the A39

Parking: Lorna Doone Car Park as per start point above

Public Transport: None. Nearest railway station is Barnstaple (17.4 miles)

Distance: 4½ miles

Refreshments: Café Deli, Malmsmead, 01643 863250, Rockford Inn, Brendon, 01598 741214; Staghunters Inn, Brendon, 01598 741222

Toilets: In the car park

Nearby places to stay: Meadpool House B&B, Brendon, 01598 741215; Rockford Inn, Brendon, 01598 741214; Staghunters Inn, Brendon, 01598 741222

Nearby places of interest: Watersmeet (National Trust), Watersmeet Rd, Lynmouth 01598 753348

Possible birds include: Blackbird, blue tit, buzzard, carrion crow, chaffinch, dipper, dunnock, goosander, great tit, grey heron, gulls of various type, house sparrow, pheasant, raven, wren

Authors' tip: Malmsmead is in the heart of *Lorna Doone* country and is a good starting point from which to explore the nearby Doone Valley. This picturesque area was made famous by R. D. Blackmore's novel published in 1869

From the car park entrance cross the lane and take the bridleway signed for Southern Wood which starts through a gate near the end of a corrugated barn. This climbs steadily to a blue waymarked gate in 250m, beyond which you continue under the trees, a lovely stretch of walking under fern-fringed, lichen-encrusted trees. The path then drops to meet a lane. Go left on this for about 20m to another bridleway going left again

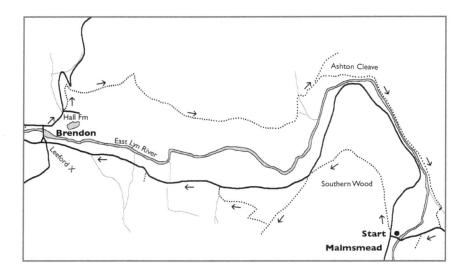

up into the trees, this is signed for Brendon Common. You climb for about 350m to emerge from the trees at a three-way fingerpost in front of a gate. Don't go through the gate but turn right on the bridleway towards Brendon, sloping woodland to your right and a lovely view ahead. The path bends right in about 150m to go under trees and winds down through the woodland, re-emerging to give a wonderful view over the valley of the East Lyn River down on the right. The path passes through a bridleway gate and just beyond you reach the lane. Turn left and follow the road for just over ½ mile to Brendon.

When you reach Leeford Green Cross you have options. The Staghunters Inn is straight ahead along the lane but the walk goes right to cross the road bridge (see feature p.78). Turn right at the end of the bridge along the lane towards Porlock. Follow this until, 200m from the bridge and after a left bend near Hall Farm, you see a clear, yellow-waymarked footpath on the right signed to County Gate and Malmsmead, 2½ miles away. Go up the steps off the lane, through the footpath gate, then up more steps, continuing ahead as the path rises to pass beneath a lovely oak tree. You reach a yellow-arrowed post about 150m from the gate. Here go sharp right, still uphill. You reach a yellow-marked gate, continue beyond this on the well-trodden path, the valley down to your right. The path continues clearly, passing another gateway and beyond this affording far reaching views across the valley, where you can see the tracks you followed earlier. Occasional yellow blobs on fence posts reassure you that you're on the right path. You start to descend, passing an occasional gate and eventually arrive at a stepped kissing gate. Continue beyond to a gate onto a footbridge. At the end of the bridge go left as indicated, the path soon bending right uphill to reach a three-way fingerpost. Go right here towards County Gate to reach a small yellow-marked gate a short distance away. A three-way fingerpost beyond the gate offers you a right hand, downhill option towards Malmsmead and Oare. Take this. The enticing Ashton Cleave is ahead of you.

The path drops steadily down and enters trees as you approach the East Lyn River. At a two-way fingerpost keep on for Malmsmead, ¾ mile away. The path is now beside the river – look out for dippers. The river bends right, pass through a yellow-marked gate to walk through the field with the river still on your right. On the far side of the field pass through another gate and continue as before, this line eventually bringing you to

Wonderful view of the East Lyn Valley

Packhorse Bridges

The lovely, humpbacked, stone bridge spanning Badgworthy Water in Malmsmead is Grade II listed and dates back to the 17thC. Such bridges were built along old trade routes to allow packhorses with their laden panniers to cross rivers more easily, the parapets usually being quite low in order  not to impede the panniers. Sometimes such bridges have recesses built into them where pedestrians can stand to avoid passing traffic, the bridges generally being quite narrow. Many such bridges have latterly been replaced by modern constructions more equal to the task of 21stC traffic although sometimes original bridges have been widened in order to cope. In Brendon the old packhorse bridge is further along the river – turn left after the road bridge to find it a short way along the lane, before resuming your walk.

Glebe House on the left, 400m after the bend in the river. During this stretch of the walk you have actually been in Somerset, the river being the boundary – we know it's a book about Devon but there was no option here, sorry!

Keep ahead after the farm, ignoring its private footbridge and passing through a gate beyond the house with the river still on your right. It was here that we saw a trio of goosander, one male and two females. You reach a confluence of rivers: Oare Water and Badgworthy Water which run into the East Lyn River. Keep ahead, it is now Oare Water to your right. You soon reach a footbridge with blue bridleway markers. Cross here and follow the path beyond to climb up past Parsonage Farm. Pass through a gate and follow the fenced path to meet the lane. Turn right along the lane and follow it back to Malmsmead. Cross the bridge or ford Badgworthy Water, as you prefer, and you will find the car park from which you started behind Lorna Doone Farm.

Ashton Cleave

Exmoor pony investigates passing walker

Whitefield Down & the Tarka Trail

Distance: 5¾ miles / 9¼km

This walk offers some breathtaking inland views and snippets of history along the way. Part of the route follows the 'paw-marked' Tarka Trail as this region was made famous in Henry Williamson's book 'Tarka the Otter'. The area has interesting associations with the village of Poltimore, near Exeter. The terrain is undulating but not extremely steep. It can be boggy in places and you may find a compass useful, though not vital as long as conditions are clear.

Map: Outdoor Leisure 9, Exmoor 1:25 000	
Start point: Yarde Down Cross – The Poltimore Arms. Grid ref: SS724356. Postcode: EX36 3HA	
Directions to start: Yarde Down Cross is east of the A399 between Brayford and Simonsbath	
Parking: On the lane in the vicinity of Yarde Down Cross and the pub. There is a wide area adjacent to the junction. Please exercise courtesy towards other road users	
Public Transport: Bus 657 operated by TT Coaches stops outside the Poltimore Arms. Timetables available online at www.travelinesw.com. Nearest railway station is Barnstaple (9 miles)	
Distance: 5¾ miles	
Refreshments: Poltimore Arms, Yarde Down, 01598 710381	
Toilets: None en route	
Nearby places to stay: Higher Riscombe Farm, Simonsbath, 01643 831713; The Old Orchard, Brayford, 01598 710256	
Nearby places of interest: Exmoor Zoological Park, South Stowford, 01598 763352. Quince Honey Farm, South Molton, 01769 572401; South Molton Museum, 01769 572951	
Possible birds include: Blackbird, buzzard, carrion crow, chaffinch, goldfinch, gulls of various type, house sparrow, pheasant, skylark, swallow, swift, snipe, starling, woodpigeon	
Authors' tip: Although not in North Devon, if you find yourself near Exeter Poltimore House is worth a visit. Check their website for details of events and open days: http://www.poltimore.org/	

From outside the Poltimore Arms turn left along the lane and left again at the T-junction which you reach almost immediately. After about 100m you reach a broad track on the left signed as a public footpath to Whitefield and Kedworthy. This is Sherracombe Lane, and is your way.

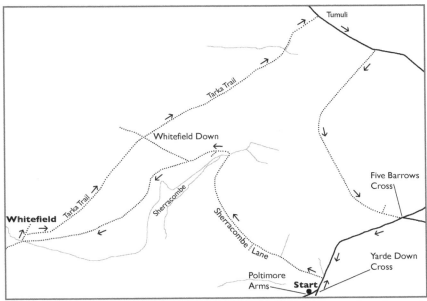

Follow the track, ignoring any gates to left or right but passing through an occasional gate across the track, until it descends to cross a stream and swings left, almost 1 mile from the lane. The track starts to climb beyond the stream. Here, the area to the right of the track was the subject of an archaeological dig some years ago and evidence of iron smelting and smithing dating from Roman times was discovered, dated by pieces of Roman pottery. About 100m after the bend the track forks; keep right, uphill.

You climb to a gateway with a yellow footpath blob and good views back the way you have come. Pass through this gate, bearing left to a kissing gate about 15m away. Go through this and follow the left hand (Whitefield) option shown on the fingerpost, heading down the field and aiming for the right hand end of a tree-lined boundary. When you reach it, follow the boundary keeping the trees to your left, down to the left is Sherracombe and the rising land to your right is Whitefield Down.

Follow this boundary for 250m. The trees come to an end but keep going beyond them until you find a two-way fingerpost. Now head obliquely right across the field, still heading for the hamlet of Whitefield, in a south westerly direction. As you crest the brow of the field a huge view lies ahead and a kissing gate with fingerpost awaits. Continue across the next field, heading very slightly south of west (the fingerpost by the gate points too far right, you need to aim slightly left of straight across). This reaches another yellow-marked gate with small fingerpost. Continue in the same line as before bearing diagonally across the field to the far left corner where you find two fingerposts directing you out of the field. Go to the lower of these, beside a gate with an adjacent stile.

Beyond the stile turn immediately right, following the fence on your right. A pale green house is down to the left. You soon join a track beside the fence, follow this, heading uphill now towards Whitefield Down. At the top of the field the track passes through a gate and continues, climb through the next field, the fence still to your right.

You reach another stile and footpath sign. Beyond here cross yet another field, passing a grass-covered brick and concrete construction to your left. There are lovely views ahead across Whitefield Down with Sherracombe to the right.

Sweeping views from the Tarka Trail

Poltimore – linking Exeter and Exmoor

North east of Exeter is the village of Poltimore, location of the vast, semi-ruined Poltimore House. John Bampfylde of Weston was gifted the Manor in 1298 by his tutor, William Pontyngton, a canon of Exeter Cathedral. The earliest part of the house dates from the Tudor period and Sir George Warwick Bampfylde, 6th Baronet, was made 'Baron Poltimore' in 1831. Although their ancestral seat was near Exeter, the family also had estates and homes in North Devon and Exmoor, hence the frequent occurrence of their name in this area. Poltimore House & Grounds are being restored by the Poltimore House Trust and make for a fascinating visit. Check the website for details of events and open days: http://www.poltimore.org/

Both photos Rikky Apps © The Friends of Poltimore House

This line brings you to a stile in the corner of the field with an adjacent four-way fingerpost. Cross the stile and keep ahead on the paw-marked Tarka Trail towards Mole's Chamber, fence to your right. Pause to glance behind – the view is good. At the top of the field is a meeting of gates. Keep ahead in the same direction, still with the fence to your right and in about 100m you reach another fingerpost beside the track.

New fencing has been installed here and the path differs slightly to what is shown on the OS map. Keep on the track, climbing steadily between fences. The track opens into a field, continue with the fence on the left. The track swings sharp left through a yellow-blobbed gate, still climbing, with the view behind ever-growing. It's worth pausing for breath as behind, on a clear day, is a sea view to Lundy.

The stony track continues uphill to the lane. Just before reaching it you see burial mounds or tumuli to either side of the path, the final resting places of the bones of our ancestors who had their being in this area. They have views to die for. Go through the gate by the fingerpost and turn right along the narrow, lofty lane for 450m until you reach a broad track on your right. Take this and follow it for over 1.5km, enjoying glorious views to the right over the countryside you covered earlier in the walk. Note the appealing mossy furriness of the 'laid' hedge flanking the track.

The track reaches a lane at Five Barrows Cross. Not far from here, in the area of the barrows, an underground bunker was constructed during the Cold War, replacing a 2nd World War army hut. The bunker was later capped over and sealed after some people tried to occupy it. Turn right down the lane heading back down to your start point less than 1km away.

Glorious views from the track leading to Five Barrows Cross

Hartland Quay & Hartland Point
Distance: 7 miles / 11¼km

The cliffscape around Hartland Quay is quite spectacular, in places appearing almost extra-terrestrial. This easy-to-follow walk affords superb views from the coast path, although in rough weather the coastal section is exposed and windy. After heavy rain some of the paths will be muddy and there are some stiff climbs. The final short section is a retrace, giving the opportunity to enjoy the superb coastal scenery in the opposite direction.

Map: OS Explorer 126, Clovelly and Hartland 1:25 000

Start point: Hartland Quay Higher Car Park. Grid ref: SS223247. Postcode: EX39 6DU

Directions to start: Hartland Quay lies 2½ miles to the west of the village of Hartland itself, the most north-westerly settlement in Devon. The village can be accessed via a combination of the A39 and B3248

Parking: Hartland Quay Higher Car Park. Post code: EX39 6DU

Public Transport: Bus operators that call at the nearby village of Hartland are: Stagecoach Devon, Jacketts Coaches and Hemmings Coaches. Timetables available online at www.travelinesw.com. The nearest railway station is Barnstaple (19 miles)

Distance: 7 miles

Refreshments: Hart Inn, The Square, Hartland, 01237 441474; Hartland Quay Hotel, 01237 441218

Toilets: At Hartland Quay

Nearby places to stay: B&B at 1 Coastguard Cottages, Stoke, 01237 441011; Blegberry B&B, Hartland, 01237 441713; Copps Castle B&B, Hartland, 01237 441733; Hartland Quay Hotel, 01237 441218

Nearby places of interest: Docton Mill Gardens, Lymebridge, Hartland, 01237 441369; Hartland Abbey, Hartland, 01237 441234

Possible birds include: Blackbird, carrion crow, gulls of various type, house sparrow, magpie, pied wagtail, raven, robin, rock pipit, starling, woodpigeon, wren

Authors' tip: We love the island of Lundy. It can be visited for a day trip as well as holidays: 01271 863636 / www.lundyisland.co.uk

Across the lane from the higher car park a two-way fingerpost directs you (in a rather random fashion) uphill along a narrow path beside the lane. The path rises to give good views to the left along the coast with Lundy out to sea. It joins a broader path coming in from the right,

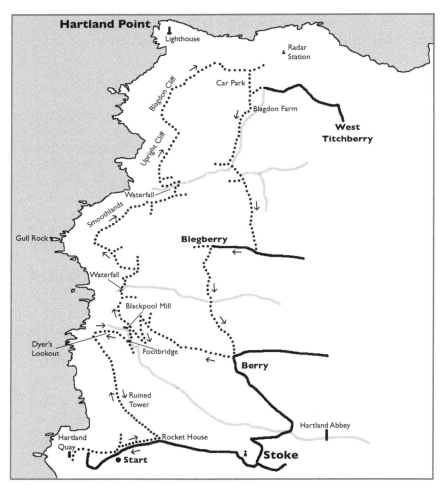

continue ahead uphill to reach Rocket House. Here go left along the coast path, as signed by the fingerpost. On some posts you will notice the coast path's acorn waymark symbol.

Walk along the clifftop, sea to your left and a ruined tower ahead: enjoy the view towards Stoke Church through its arch. 600m from Rocket House the path drops to a two-way fingerpost with a badge denoting Dyer's Lookout. Follow the coast path beyond here, descending to cross a stream and eventually reaching Blackpool Mill, which was used as a location in the BBC's costume drama *Sense and Sensibility* in 2007 and also in the 2006 mini-series of Rosamunde Pilcher's *The Shell Seekers*.

Beyond here ascend a flight of steps up the cliff. At the top you will be rewarded by a beautiful view of waterfalls cascading to the beach in the cove below. Your way now follows the coast path for almost 2 miles until you reach the cliffs above the lighthouse at Hartland Point. On the way you will, from time to time, pass footpaths heading inland which should be ignored, although occasionally you will find the coast path itself is out of sight of the sea as it wends its way behind high cliffs. It takes you past stretches of coast known as Smoothlands, Upright Cliff and Blagdon and just before Hartland Point you reach a memorial stone to the people on the hospital ship Glenart Castle which was torpedoed in 1918. There's a good view down to the lighthouse from this vantage point. Continue past a mast and its adjacent building, still following the coast path towards the noticeable Civil Aviation Authority radar beacon with its blobby top. The path becomes surfaced and leads into an area of car park. Walk through this and at its far end turn right on a tarmac drive, heading inland and leaving the coast path.

The view from Hartland Quay

The dramatic coastline of Hartland

Soon you pass the Heliport which serves Lundy and where you may see alpacas grazing. Just beyond this look out for the three-way fingerpost. From here keep straight on along the bridleway for Blegberry, which passes farm buildings and descends to pass a house followed by more barns. Follow the blue bridleway arrows along the track, which enters a field – keep ahead beside the right hand hedge. At the end of the field continue on the track for 100m to a three-way fingerpost. Here go left, still on the path to Blegberry. The path quickly crosses a stream and passes through a gate, then bears right and crosses a footbridge. Continue on, ignoring the yellow-arrowed footpath going right soon after the bridge. The track continues for a further 560m before emerging through a gate onto a broader track. Here turn right for a few metres to reach the lane.

Go right along the lane and soon you arrive at the buildings of Blegberry Farm where you will find a two-way fingerpost. Go left here on the unmetalled road, which is in fact tarmac until it has passed a couple of houses. Beyond these the track continues downhill. Follow it for 700m until you reach a lane at its bend. Go right here, to join another track signed as public footpath.

You're now heading back towards the coast. Eventually the track enters a field. Continue beside the right hand hedge for 240m descending with the track, and as it bends distinctly right look for the post with two yellow arrows. Follow the direction of the one pointing left off the track, now walking down a field for just over 100m until you find another post with an arrow pointing sharply left downhill. Follow this path as it descends between gorse bushes, the coast to your right.

You reach a yellow-arrowed gate. Continue beyond it until you drop to meet a two-way fingerpost on a broad track, this is 200m from the sharp left turn above. Turn right here, heading down to Blackpool Mill Cottage again. Here you see a three-way fingerpost. Go left towards Hartland Quay, retracing your steps a short way through the field, following the yellow arrow to re-cross the stream.

Stoke Church framed by ruin

Beyond the river you reach another three-way fingerpost. Go right along the coast path back towards Hartland Quay, passing the ruined tower before reaching Rocket House. This is a beautiful stretch of the walk and different in reverse! At Rocket House join the lane and turn right along it – the easy option back to the car park.

Lundy

Three miles long by just over half a mile wide this island has a colourful history despite its small size. Evidence of occupation harks back to Neolithic times. Owned by the Marisco family in the 13thC, after whom the tavern is named, it has also been the haunt of pirates and, during the 18thC, the unofficial  'residence' of deported convicts. The Harman family owned it during the early 20thC and in 1969 sold it to Jack Hayward who gave the island to The National Trust, the present owners. Lundy's holiday accommodation is administered by the Landmark Trust and it makes for a beautiful destination – a glorious place for bird watching, rock climbing, walking and diving amongst many other appeals. 'Lund-e' is old Norse for 'puffin island' and although the puffin population is now quite minimal you may still be lucky enough to see them in spring off the west coast.

The unspoilt location of Blackpool Mill

Hartland Point

Great Torrington
Distance: 2 miles / 3.2km

A short walk enjoying some beautiful inland views and interesting history. There are ascents, but it is the most well-benched walk we know if you need a breather. The stretch beside the river might be muddy, but the walk is generally on good paths. Otters live hereabouts but you are unlikely to see them.

Map: OS Explorer 126, Clovelly and Hartland 1:25 000

Start point: Sydney House Car Park, South Street. Grid ref: SS494189. Postcode: EX38 8AA

Directions to start: Great Torrington lies 12½ miles south west of Barnstaple in North Devon. The A386 leads into the town

Parking: Sydney House Car Park, South Street. Post code: EX38 8AA

Public Transport: Great Torrington is served by buses from many local towns. These are operated by Beacon Bus, Stagecoach Devon and Turners Tours. Timetables available online at www.travelinesw.com. Nearest railway station is Chapelton (6.8 miles)

Distance: 2 miles

Refreshments: Brown's Delicatessen, 37 South Street, 01805 622900; Café @ Torrington 1646, Castle Hill, 01805 626146; The Plough Arts Centre Café, 9–11 Fore Street, 01805 625925

Toilets: Sydney House Car Park and pannier market

Nearby places to stay: Broadpark Breaks B&B, Frithelstock, Great Torrington, 01805 622214; Higher Darracott Farm, nr Huntshaw, 01805 622621; Way Barton B&B, Sherwood Green Cross, St. Giles in the Wood, 01769 560569

Nearby places of interest: Dartington Crystal, Linden Close, 01805 626242; Torrington 1646, Castle Hill, South Street, 01805 626146; RHS Garden Rosemoor (just outside Great Torrington on the A3124), 01805 624067

Possible birds include: Blackbird, buzzard, carrion crow, gulls of various type, jackdaw, pheasant, pied wagtail, robin, starling, woodpigeon, wren

Authors' tip: The historic St. Michael and All Angels Church is worth a visit (see feature p.95)

Start at the back of the car park overlooking the Torridge Valley. If you get no further it's worth coming to Torrington just for this view. Below you to the right is the village of Taddiport and to the left of the village you will see the historic 'strip' fields.

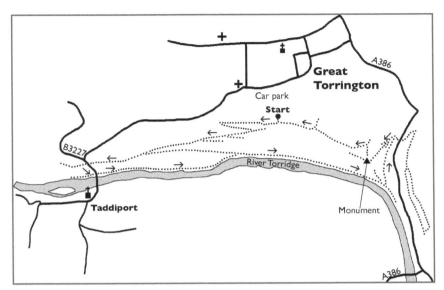

Leave your car to enjoy the view and at the back left corner of the car park seek the gateway, low down in the surrounding stone wall. Go through here and turn right along the path, with the wall on your right and the vast view to your left. This narrow path is the Old Maid's Walk. Follow it as it bends sharply left down steps. You soon meet another descending path, turn sharp right along it and continue downhill, staying on this path and ignoring any others to left or right. The river is down to your left and you are gradually getting closer to it. At the bottom you pass a stone plinth telling you this is the Millennium Path, beyond which you meet a broad track. Turn right along it.

The track immediately forks, keep left on the path nearest the river, which is still below to your left at this point. You reach the lane, turn left along it, passing the Old Toll House and a public footpath stile on the left, to reach Taddiport Bridge. Enjoy the river views from here then retrace your steps a few metres back to the stile, turning right off the lane to walk through the field beside the river, which is now to your right. This is a lovely stretch of the walk.

At the end of the field turn left away from the river to a gap in the fence. Go through here to meet a broad track, but rather than following the track go immediately right down a narrow path that passes through a chicane of metal fencing. Walk ahead beyond here and you'll soon find yourself on a delightful, narrow path under trees beside the river. Don't slide in.

You will eventually see steps going up left to join the track above you. Ignore the first flight but take the second, as the narrow path becomes rather less navigable after this. Turn right at the top of the steps and follow the track until, when the river bends right and about 750m from the metal chicane, you find a broad path coming down from the left. Turn left up this, you will probably hear traffic as you are now approaching the road above you. If it hasn't dried up, look out for the attractive cascade of small waterfalls along the stream to the right of this rising path. The path ascends to meet a flight of steps ahead, just before which you will see a plinth naming this path 'Lady Wash'. Climb the steps and turn left along the path at their top, walking away from the road. Ignore the almost-immediate left fork and keep ahead, climbing gently on this narrow, well-surfaced path and ignoring any other paths off until you rise to meet the Monument, erected in June 1818 to commemorate the

View over the Torridge Valley close to the start point

Monument to commemorate the Battle of Waterloo

Great Torrington

The unusual, narrow fields in the valley are now all that remain of an old mediæval farming system which was used by inmates of the leper hospital at Taddiport (meaning 'toad gate') which existed during the 13th–14thC. These fields enabled the patients to grow their own food. Later, during the English Civil  War, Torrington was a very active place. It was first a stronghold for Royalist troops under Lord Hopton. Thomas Fairfax brought their stand to an end in 1646 when the town was taken at the Battle of Torrington. Unbeknown to Fairfax, the Royalists had been using the church to store gunpowder and a stray spark ignited this, blowing the roof off the church where Fairfax had housed his prisoners. Sadly they, and many of Fairfax's men, were killed. The victims are buried under a big cobbled mound outside the church.

Scenic bench stops abound on this walk

Battle of Waterloo. Savour the fabulous views from here. Also, stand close and look straight up the edifice at the tufts of ivy-leaved toadflax softening its edges against the sky.

From here take the good path heading **away** from the view, George's Path. Stay on this as it climbs to a left bend at which point you find a memorial bench to George Charles Stacey for whom the path is named. Continue on his path, now walking with the airy view to your left once more. At the end of George's Path continue along the row of well-placed benches, dating from various mayoralty incumbencies, and beyond them rejoin the path below the lofty car park wall. Follow this back to the gate through which you started the walk earlier.